A Woman of Valour

Our Lives: DIARY, MEMOIR, AND LETTERS
Series Editor: Janice Dickin

Our Lives aims at both student and general readership.

Today's students, living in a world of blogs, understand that there is much to be learned from the everyday lives of everyday people. *Our Lives* seeks to make available previously unheard voices from the past and present. Social history in general contests the construction of history as the story of elites and the act of making available the lives of everyday people, as seen by themselves, subverts even further the contentions of social historiography.

At the same time, *Our Lives* aims to make available books that are good reads. General readers are guaranteed quality, provided with introductions that they can use to contextualize material and are given a glimpse of other works they might want to look at. It is not usual for university presses to provide this type of primary material. Athabasca University considers provision of this sort of material as important to its role as Canada's Open University.

SERIES TITLES

A Woman of Valour

THE BIOGRAPHY OF
MARIE-LOUISE BOUCHARD LABELLE

by Claire Trépanier

translated from the French
by Louise Mantha

AU PRESS
Athabasca University

Originally published as *C'est le temps d'en parler* by AU Press
and Éditions Carte blanche

© 2009 Claire Trépanier
© 2010 Claire Trépanier

Published by AU Press, Athabasca University
1200, 10011–109 Street   Edmonton, AB   T5J 3S8

Library and Archives Canada Cataloguing in Publication

Trépanier, Claire, 1949–
     A woman of valour : the biography of Marie-Louise Bouchard Labelle /
by Claire Trépanier.

Translation of: C'est le temps d'en parler.
Includes bibliographical references and index.
Also available in electronic format (978-1-897425-85-5).
ISBN 978-1-897425-84-8

1. Roy, Marie-Louise, 1891–1973. 2. Roy, Jérémie Alphonse, 1858–1944.
3. Ottawa (Ont.)--Biography. 4. Catholic Church--Ontario--Clergy--Biography.
5. Catholic Church--Clergy--Family relationships--Ontario. I. Title.

FC3096.26.L32T7413 2010   971.3'8404092   C2010-900883-9

Cover design by Rod Michalchuk, General Idea.
Printed and bound in Canada by Marquis Book Printing.

The author may be contacted by email at pourenparler@sympatico.ca.

À Marie‑Louise.

C'est le temps d'en parler.

CONTENTS

Foreword

AN ORDINARY LIFE

The story I am about to tell here is that of one of those women who lived an "ordinary" life, that is, a life that would not be included in the official history of the country nor cause a stir in the community, at least not on the surface.

However, when we start questioning people who have lived a so-called ordinary life, one sometimes discovers stories that are far from ordinary. The story of Marie-Louise Bouchard Labelle is such a one. To live an illegitimate love with a priest thirty-three years older than oneself, survive the Great Depression of the early twentieth century as a single parent, and launch into business barely knowing how to read or write, does not correspond with the images that one normally associates with an ordinary life. In her ongoing struggle to survive and to raise her three children, Marie-Louise showed ingenuity, determination, generosity and joie de vivre. Her story is that of an ordinary life of great interest.

BOOK METHODOLOGY

Many challenges confronted me as I embarked on the adventure of writing this biography. First of all, it was the story of a deceased woman that I had never known. Furthermore, since she was practically illiterate, she did not leave behind significant written documents such as a diary or a sustained correspondence with someone. Finally, she had promised her loved one to never speak of their life together, with the result that she took to her grave the details of their love story, leaving a great part of her life in the dark. To learn about her story, I interviewed her children, her grandchildren and other family members. Many sketches of Marie-Louise's personality emerged through these interviews, each person having known her at different periods in her life. Since they are the ones who told me her story, I have chosen to let them speak for themselves. Their words can describe better than mine the mentality of the day, the local humour and the richness of Marie-Louise's relationships with people in her environment.

A BILINGUAL BOOK

The original French version of this book contained quotes in English because its story stems from a bilingual reality. Marie-Louise was born in the Province of Quebec, therefore in a French-speaking milieu. She lived in a small francophone enclave in northern Ontario where, in the late nineteenth century, economic development was mostly the purview of anglophone masters. Although the father of Marie-Louise's children was a French Canadian with a true French name, through the whimsies of destiny her children were raised with an English name. The interviews I conducted with Marie-Louise's immediate and extended family took place sometimes in French, sometimes in English, and sometimes in both languages.

In the original version of the book, I chose to keep in English the parts of the interviews conducted in English so as not to lose the local colour of the language and of the emotions expressed by the interviewees. Another reason motivated me as well: the reality of our country. It is said repeatedly that "two solitudes" are living parallel lives in this country. However, the reality is that francophones and anglophones brush up against each other daily. They work together, exchange ideas, maintain friendships and often enjoy leisure activities with one another. Intercultural marriages are multiplying. In respecting the language of my interviewees, the original version of the book reflected that reality, that is to say, the bilingual character of one nation where, in its diversity, people can create love bonds that transcend all linguistic barriers.

Claire Trépanier
Ottawa, February 2008

Editor's notes regarding translations:
Unless otherwise noted, all translation of the text, quotes, appendixes and notes is by Louise Mantha.

Direct quotes that are set in italics in this book are translated from the French. Direct quotes not in italics indicate text that was in English in the original French version of the book, *C'est le temps d'en parler.*

Acknowledgements

I wish to thank Gertrude Mantha, Marie-Louise's daughter, who was my dear companion, my principal source of information and my constant support. Her confidence in me kept me motivated throughout the entire project. I will be eternally grateful to Louise Mantha who, in suggesting one evening in January 2004 that I write her grandmother's story, stimulated me to pursue a lifelong dream, that of writing a biography. And Louise, thank you for accepting to translate this book into English and for investing in this task not only your language skills but also all the emotions this story stirred in your heart.

I thank all those who accepted to be interviewed for their sincerity, their open-mindedness and for the interesting stories they told me. I am enormously in debt to those who assisted me in my research and whose names appear in an appendix. A special thank you to Lynn Keating in Wolseley, Saskatchewan for having rummaged in the archives of the little Saint Anne's church to find the photo of Father Roy, and having given me the name of a Canadian priest on secondment to the Vatican: precious information for me. Thanks also to Sister Ria Gerritsen, then archivist in the Regina archdiocese, who found Father Roy's correspondence with his Bishop, Monsignor Langevin, and allowed me to photocopy it. To all the members of Marie-Louise's family, I express my sincere gratitude for having leant me photographs. The latter allow readers to put faces to the names and enrich the biography.

Sincere thanks as well to Carol Quimper who, from London

England, edited my manuscript word by word and line by line to ensure the quality of the grammar, and who worked weekends so as to give it back to me sooner. Carol, your husband must clench his teeth when my name is mentioned! Many thanks to Solange Deschênes, reviewer, and to Juliette Champagne, who both gave me useful suggestions for improving the text.

I am especially grateful to Dr. Frits Pannekoek, President of Athabasca University (AU), to Mr. Walter Hildebrandt, Director of the Athabasca University Press (AUP), and to Dr. Janice Dickin, editor of the Press' memoir series, who all expressed interest in my manuscript and encouraged me to submit it to AUP's editorial committee for review. My heartfelt thanks go to Renata Brunner Jass, Senior Editor, who edited the English version of this book, and to Tiffany Foster and Linda Kadis for the production and promotion of the book.

Finally, I could not have completed this project without the unconditional support from my guardian angel of a husband, Peter Homulos, who established some contacts for me, built the itinerary of our vacation across Canada around my research, and who more than once gently brought me back to the task when the discipline of writing every day got too onerous and I was tempted to stray for an afternoon. Thank you for your love, generous, intuitive and constant. I love you.

Claire Trépanier
Ottawa, February 2008

Preface

When my daughter, Louise, came to me three years ago with the idea that her friend Claire might be interested in writing a story about my mother, I felt strange and frightened. Everything in my early family life had been a secret for so long that I felt it was more than I could handle to accept to do the project. But the story of what my mother had gone through and everything she did to survive should be told.

In doing her research and interviewing me, Claire was so patient and understanding. Now that the book is finished, I feel relieved: after all these years, the things that were bottled up are now out in the open. It has taken a load off my mind, and I feel a sense of release. So much has gone on with the Catholic Church that has disturbed people's lives ... it is time to come out in the open. Talking about my story will maybe bring the same sense of relief to other people who are in the same boat.

I hope that all who read this book will see what an extraordinary woman my mother was. With very little, she did her utmost to ensure her children's survival and happiness. I appreciate all her efforts and I still love her very much.

In writing this book, Claire Trépanier helped me better understand my past. I am extremely relieved, and I owe her more than I can say.

Gertrude Mantha
August 2007

Family of Georgianne Tremblay and her two spouses

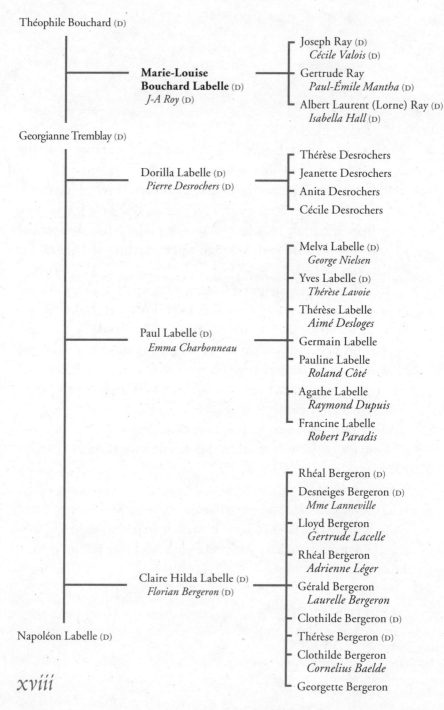

Théophile Bouchard (D)

Georgianne Tremblay (D)

Napoléon Labelle (D)

Marie-Louise Bouchard Labelle (D)
J-A Roy (D)

- Joseph Ray (D)
  Cécile Valois (D)
- Gertrude Ray
  Paul-Émile Mantha (D)
- Albert Laurent (Lorne) Ray (D)
  Isabella Hall (D)

Dorilla Labelle (D)
Pierre Desrochers (D)

- Thérèse Desrochers
- Jeanette Desrochers
- Anita Desrochers
- Cécile Desrochers

Paul Labelle (D)
Emma Charbonneau

- Melva Labelle (D)
  George Nielsen
- Yves Labelle (D)
  Thérèse Lavoie
- Thérèse Labelle
  Aimé Desloges
- Germain Labelle
- Pauline Labelle
  Roland Côté
- Agathe Labelle
  Raymond Dupuis
- Francine Labelle
  Robert Paradis

Claire Hilda Labelle (D)
Florian Bergeron (D)

- Rhéal Bergeron (D)
- Desneiges Bergeron (D)
  Mme Lanneville
- Lloyd Bergeron
  Gertrude Lacelle
- Rhéal Bergeron
  Adrienne Léger
- Gérald Bergeron
  Laurelle Bergeron
- Clothilde Bergeron (D)
- Thérèse Bergeron (D)
- Clothilde Bergeron
  Cornelius Baelde
- Georgette Bergeron

xviii

Family of Marie=Louise Bouchard Labelle and Joseph Ray

**Marie-Louise
Bouchard Labelle** (D)

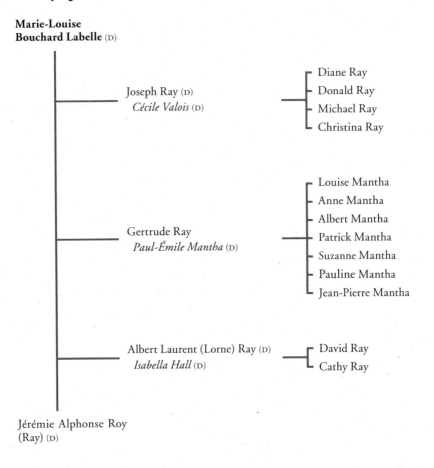

Joseph Ray (D)
Cécile Valois (D)

Diane Ray
Donald Ray
Michael Ray
Christina Ray

Gertrude Ray
Paul-Émile Mantha (D)

Louise Mantha
Anne Mantha
Albert Mantha
Patrick Mantha
Suzanne Mantha
Pauline Mantha
Jean-Pierre Mantha

Albert Laurent (Lorne) Ray (D)
Isabella Hall (D)

David Ray
Cathy Ray

Jérémie Alphonse Roy
(Ray) (D)

(D) = DECEASED

PROLOGUE

Marie-Louise Bouchard Labelle, an unmarried 25-year-old woman living in her parents' home in Hanmer, Ontario, discovers that she is pregnant by a 58-year-old priest from Cache Bay. She is fraught with questions. Who can she turn to? Should she confide this terrible secret to her parents? Will they renounce her forever? Will they become the shame of Hanmer? And what will her lover say? The decision she came to after what seemed an eternity of deliberations will forever alter the course of her life.

CHAPTER ONE

1891 TO 1906

From Les Escoumins to Hanmer

*I learned Nanny's story the day
I got married. I was 23 years old.
My Mother said, "I must talk to you."
I thought she was going to tell me
about sex, you know, at age 23!
But she wanted to tell me the story
of my grandmother and grandfather.*

~ LOUISE MANTHA

My mother was born in a place called Escoumins and it is at the mouth of the Saguenay River, way up, way past Québec city. Anyhow, she was born there and her father was a Bouchard, Théophile Bouchard, and her mother was Georgina Tremblay. Tremblay originated from Lac-Saint-Jean.[1]

I am interviewing Mrs. Gertrude Mantha, the daughter of Marie-Louise Bouchard Labelle. She is 87 years old and, as I write these words, the sole survivor of Marie-Louise's three children. It is not without reluctance that Gertrude has allowed me to write her mother's story. In a recorded text that she gave to me, she started off by saying:

> *I question whether or not I am doing the right thing because my mother kept her secret right to the end of her life at age 82 and so I wonder if maybe I shouldn't talk about all that ... anyway, I suppose we could do this with ... without using names.*[2]

She is afraid to stir up stories that could make some people lose face or could hurt the pride of others. She doesn't want to offend anyone but, at the same time, she thinks it is important that her children know their grandmother's story and that her grandchildren know that of their great-grandmother. Gertrude is a gentle woman, with a well-honed sense of humour. She speaks to me sometimes in English and sometimes in French as she recounts her memories.

She shows me her mother Marie-Louise's baptismal certificate. It indicates that Marie-Louise's mother was called Georgianne Tremblay. Since the transfer of information was done more orally than by writing in those days, names frequently underwent slight changes throughout the years. So, in her family she was affectionately known as Georgie (Georger in French), even though her baptismal certificate stated Georgianne. On her tombstone, it is written Georgina. When she gave birth to Marie-Louise, in Les Escoumins in the Province of Quebec on 30 September 1891, Georgianne could never have imagined in her wildest dreams that one day this child would defy society and the Catholic Church by choosing a lifestyle considered unacceptable for a woman in the early twentieth century in Canada.

In 1891, the village of Les Escoumins is only a small group of homes bordering a lovely bay on the north shore of the Saint Lawrence River. But it already had a long history. According to archaeological research, native North Americans would have resided here 6,000 years ago. Later, *"Basque hunters and fishermen, attracted by the cod and whale stocks, would have stopped here many times from approximately 1550 onwards."* [3] It is only in 1825 that a first white settler would have set up a permanent residence as an employee of the Hudson's Bay Company. Since then, Les Escoumins went on to become the haven of many families with old French-Canadian roots, such as the Tremblays from Lac Saint Jean, Marie-Louise's family. Thus Marie-Louise first saw the light of day in a community with a profound cultural heritage.

The baptismal registry for Saint-Marcellin Parish indicates that Marie-Louise's father, Théophile Bouchard, works as a day labourer and is absent for the christening. The forest industry, naval construction, agriculture and fishing constitute the backbone of the regional economy. The document does not indicate in what kind of trade Théophile is engaged but I imagine that, bent over his work on the morning of 1 October 1891, he thinks about his future responsibilities as a breadwinner while Georgianne makes her way to the baptismal font with their baby girl in her arms.

The baptismal registry also testifies that the baby's uncle, Jean Bouchard, and his wife Catherine Dion, attend the ceremony as godfather and godmother. They will not have the pleasure of seeing their godchild grow up in their community, for Théophile has heard that they are hiring in the mines at Copper Cliff, near Sudbury, and only a few years after Marie-Louise's birth, he moves there with his family to try and improve their standard of living.

The Bouchards are not seen as eccentric in immigrating to Ontario. In the nineteenth century, Quebec's economy undergoes a gradual and profound transformation. The province changes from a rural economy to an industrial one. This metamorphosis causes much unemployment *and at the end of the century, one counts almost* 100,000 *Quebecers who choose to emigrate to other Canadian provinces, mainly to Ontario.*"[4]

But while work in northern Ontario mines ensures a slightly improved income, it involves greater dangers. In 1893, Théophile dies in Copper Cliff, victim of an accident in the open-air foundry where he is working. The *Sudbury Journal* of 2 November covers the event:

> On Friday last, while blasting was going on at the roast beds, a premature discharge took place, one man, Tuffield (lit.) Bouchard, being so terribly injured that he died on Wednesday morning. Both eyes were blown out, and his face and hands completely blackened and shattered. Another, Geo. Tremblay, was also seriously injured, but will recover. Bouchard leaves a wife and family; the other was unmarried.[5]

Georgianne learns about her husband's demise from a young man named Napoléon Labelle who works in the same foundry. Georgette Bergeron, Napoléon's granddaughter, tells me:

In Copper Cliff, apparently my grandfather was "the boss" of Mr. Bouchard, Georgie's first husband. ... And that is how Napoléon first met Georgie, so my mother told us. As the foreman, it was his job to go tell the widow that her husband had died.[6]

For a young widow with a 2-year-old baby, earning a living in a mining town can be brutal. Georgianne cannot consider staying alone in Copper Cliff. So she decides to move in with her brother, Georges Tremblay, who lives with his wife in Capreol, north of Sudbury. For her sister-in-law, the unexpected arrival in her household of this mother and her baby surely brings about important changes. However, I imagine that she soon comes to appreciate the company of the newcomer and her help with daily chores. Anyway, Georgianne's stay at her brother's does not last long.

Marie-Louise Bouchard as a child

MARIE-LOUISE LABELLE

Indeed, Napoléon Labelle has not forgotten the pretty widow. He seeks and finds many excuses to go and visit her in Capreol and soon he is courting her. Twenty-eight years old, tall, sturdy with a full moustache, Napoléon is a handsome man. He has plans for the future and, during his visits, he probably shares them with Georgianne. He is thinking of leaving the foundry where he works. He would like to take advantage of the Ontario Government's offer, which to encourage development in New Ontario is selling land for 50 cents an acre, in return for certain conditions. He would have to clear the land, of course, but after a few years he would be owner of a beautiful farm in a new community. He would finally be master of his financial future instead of depending on the limited salary from the foundry. Would Georgianne be ready to adopt the lifestyle of a pioneer for a few years? She thinks about her daughter's future. She does not fear hard work and she is anxious to have her own home. Napoléon's dream appeals to her very much. Thus, Georgianne and Napoléon get married on 13 May 1895 in Saint Anne's Parish in Sudbury and take up residence in Copper Cliff. Little Marie-Louise, born Bouchard, acquires the surname of her adoptive father and becomes Marie-Louise Labelle.

ARRIVAL IN HANMER

Right after his wedding, Napoléon and three other settlers go to Hanmer and start clearing their recently acquired wooded lots to turn them into arable land. They return to Copper Cliff to spend the winter. Tales of their hard work must surely spice up conversation during the long winter nights, with optimists predicting the eventual establishment of a whole new community and envious people calculating the possibilities of a failure. The four men do not let themselves be discouraged by the difficulties of the work.

For three summers in a row they return to Hanmer to complete the clearing of their lots.

Meanwhile, Georgianne is keeping house in Copper Cliff, slowly introducing Marie-Louise to domestic work. In January 1898, she is pregnant again. Marie-Louise is 7 years old. The notion of having a new baby sister or brother undoubtedly pleases her. It will be a playmate in this world of adults, someone with whom to share her dreams and secrets.

On 29 April 1898, Napoléon and his three companions arrive in Hanmer to settle permanently, thereby giving rise to a small community and establishing a milestone in the history of New Ontario.[7] Georgianne and Marie-Louise do not move to Hanmer with Napoléon right away. As Georgianne is pregnant, Napoléon prefers that she stay in Copper Cliff with Marie-Louise until the birth of the baby due in October. He takes advantage of the summer months to build the family homestead and to make necessary provisions to face their first winter in Hanmer. On 15 October 1898, Georgianne gives birth to a girl, Claire-Hilda, who will simply be called Claire in daily life. Marie-Louise is delighted to have a little sister and all her life will maintain a special bond with her.

In December, Napoléon returns to Copper Cliff to fetch Georgianne, Marie-Louise and Claire. Later, DesNeiges Bergeron, Napoléon's granddaughter, will write in *Pionnières de chez nous*:

> *It was in early December, the best time to travel since the roads were frozen.... During the trip, Claire had her first slide in the snow; the carriage overturned but the baby was unharmed.*[8]

LIFE OF HANMER'S FIRST SETTLERS

The life awaiting the four settlers and their families in Hanmer is not recommended for wimps! *"One has to walk four kilometres to*

get drinking water" and *"walk a distance of approximately thirty ki-*
lometres round-trip on the path from Hanmer to Copper Cliff" [9] to
buy basic supplies. Winters are hard and provisions scarce. Shelters
for the few farm animals come down to tree trunks tied at the top
and fanned out at the bottom. In springtime, the dirt roads are
transformed into mud furrows, making transportation difficult. In
summertime, flies relentlessly attack both workers and livestock.
However, these difficulties do not discourage the pioneers. They
have the independence for which they had hoped. They are now
masters of their own destiny, masters of all decisions concerning
their lands and their community.

The information that I found about the dwelling awaiting
Georgianne and her children on their arrival in Hanmer in 1898
differs from one source to another. In the book *Pionnières de
chez nous* it states that the abode was made of logs and had only
"three triangular sides." [10] During my interview with Clothilde
Bergeron, Georgianne's granddaughter, I asked her about this
curious house:

> **C.T.:** *What did a three-sided house look like?*
> **C.B.:** *Well, they built walls on the north, east and*
> *west sides and left open the southern side. During*
> *the winter, they would put up panels in the front*
> *to stay warm and leave a small space for the door.*
> *They built a fire in the doorway to cook their*
> *meals. It warmed them up.* [11]

There is consensus between Clothilde and other members of her
family that Napoléon and Georgianne did not live in a three-sided
house. As they were moving in with two children, one of them just
a two month old baby, Napoléon would have built an ordinary
logwood house in accordance with building methods of the time.
Furthermore, he would have built the furniture. [12]

If men build the dwelling, it is women who, through long hours of hard work, turn them into homes. Their presence is essential to the family's survival. Everything must be done: disinfect the wood beds with turpentine, make straw mattresses, sew clothes for the whole family, cook and bake, feed the livestock, cultivate a garden, can preserves, help butcher animals for the winter, and, in season, pick wild berries to make pastry and jams. Add to that the preparation of celebrations such as Christmas and New Year's and, later on, when a little community has been established in Hanmer, assistance with special occasions such as weddings and christenings. Can we really understand the lives of these women who, through all this work, went through repeated pregnancies, gave birth without medical surveillance, and often took care of their children alone when their husbands had to go away to get supplies in Copper Cliff, sometimes even in Sudbury, on trips that could take several days?

Claire-Hilda (seated) and Marie-Louise Labelle, circa 1899

MARIE-LOUISE'S EDUCATION

On her arrival in Hanmer in 1898, Marie-Louise is 7 years old. She does not attend school as the Hanmer School will not be built until 1902. She is old enough to help her mother with the daily chores: wash dishes, peel potatoes, watch over baby Claire, bring in small firewood for the stove, feed the animals and weed the garden. She learns the rudiments of cooking and is gradually initiated into knitting and sewing during the long winter evenings.

Although she lives in a colonization environment, her education is not all that different from that of other young girls her age in cities in Quebec and Ontario. *"In the pre-industrial age ... the education given to young girls is limited to providing them with practical knowledge that can serve them throughout their life."* [13] Since a young girl is expected to live in the bosom of her family, learning to read and write is not considered a great necessity — a hobby at the most. But which young woman could need a hobby in days so filled with domestic chores? So the essential techniques of cooking, sewing, gardening and child care are what is extolled. This concept of a young girl's education is strongly promoted by the Catholic Church, judging from an article of Father Alfred Emery in the parish bulletin of Paincourt in 1914. He suggests adopting the following principles for the education of young girls:

> *What we must teach young girls is to have an appropriate self-confidence. We must teach them how to make bread, sew shirts and how to check and balance the accounts of their suppliers. Teach them to wear thick, sensible shoes. Bring them up according to their rank. Show them how to wash and iron clothes and to sew their own dresses. Teach them that in one dollar there are only 100 cents. Teach them to cook all kinds of food. Show them how to darn socks and sew on buttons. Teach them what constitutes good common sense*

and how to say appropriately yes or no and to not veer
from that course. Show them how to wear with dignity
a simple Indian dress and give them a good, solid educa-
tion. Teach them to put more stock in the inner qualities
than the riches of would-be suitors. Initiate them thor-
oughly in the mysteries of the kitchen, the dining room
and the living room. Make them understand that when
you spend less than you make, the difference becomes
savings. Teach them that the more you live above your
means the more you are heading to poverty. Don't forget
that their future happiness depends mainly on the ad-
vice you will give them. Teach them that one solid and
capable labourer is worth more than a dozen dandies
in suits. Introduce them to learning music, painting,
and drawing if you have the time and the means, but
make sure that they are talented above all in the art of
tending a home and of being charming and loyal.[14]

Marie-Louise's parents already apply these principles imbued with Christian values. And, even though these teachings make a lot of sense in a settlers' milieu where women try very hard to manage the household with very limited means, they do not prepare them for adapting to the changes already sprouting in the new economy. But who in this pioneer environment can foresee that one day Marie-Louise will be thrust into the labour market in the country's capital with her only education being *"the art of tending a home and of being charming and loyal"*?

PRIMARY SCHOOL

Thus Marie-Louise grows up in Hanmer following the rhythm of her daily chores. The hamlet is developing gradually. A post office was built, then a small school. A historical document found in Hanmer tells how they came to make the decision to build the school: *"In November 1902, the taxpayers of Hanmer's third conces- sion, seeing that their numerous children were growing up without any education, convened a meeting in Mr. Beaulieu's house to discuss the building of a school. The current site was offered free of charge by Mr. Jacob Proulx and it was accepted as being the most convenient for all parties. They started construction right away."* [15]

Marie-Louise is 11 years old. Her father, Napoléon, *"made all the student's desks by hand. They were really tables with a shelf for books and long benches. He also built the teacher's desk."* [16]

The first school teacher, Miss Hotte, boards with the Labelle family upon her arrival from Chelmsford. She stays with them during her whole first year in Hanmer. Marie-Louise attends the small logwood school only sporadically because she is inheriting a constantly increasing share of domestic responsibilities. The family has grown with the birth of a brother, Paul (Napoléon Junior) on 8 October 1900, and that of a sister, Dorilla, on 19 August 1903.[17] Georgianne needs more and more help at home. Gertrude, Marie-Louise's daughter, tells me:

> **G:** *Her mother was always sick, so her parents kept her at home to take care of her step-sisters and step-brothers.*
> **C:** *Did she know how to read and write?*
> **G:** *She only had limited knowledge, very little, so she had a lot of difficulty writing and also reading, you know.*[18]

Miss Hotte surely gives a few private lessons to Marie-Louise dur- ing her year-long stay with the family but Marie-Louise has very little time to devote to learning how to read and write. This lack of formal education will become a serious handicap later on when, as an adult, she finds herself suddenly and without any preparation obliged to earn her living.

TOUGH LOVE

Marie-Louise's adoptive father, Napoléon, is indisputably the head of the family. He exercises his paternal authority with a mixture of firmness and generous but reserved love. His children and his grandchildren are a little afraid of him. His pride is equalled only by his fiery temper and the children sometimes take the brunt of his outbursts. One of his granddaughters remembers:

> *When he said, "Son of a bitch!", we ran. We disappeared. And if something didn't suit him, he slapped us right away.*

And she adds:

> *Mostly, he was a very proud man. ... You didn't go to town if your moustache was not cut just so. One day, he had burned his moustache a little so he didn't go to town until the next week."* [19]

Napoléon Labelle, adoptive father of Marie-Louise

If he insists that children share the daily household chores, he also ensures that their days of work alternate with days of fun activities. Sometimes in the summer he brings them to picnic at Aylmer Lake, a few miles from home. These picnics are not simple round-trip affairs. Georgette explains me to as we drive towards the lake:

> *These roads were nothing but rabbit trails, as we say. So, if it was a little muddy, they could get stuck. And when they came here, it was also to pick blueberries. So they were coming here with a wagon and two horses, they brought tents and they stayed maybe two or three days. They slept in the tent. And they cooked outside over a fire. They picked blueberries and brought them home on the wagon. And they made preserves, one way or another. But it wasn't just next door."*[20]

So Napoléon knows how to combine business with pleasure. The children can relax and have a good time all the while assuming some responsibilities that contribute to the well-being of the entire family. Just like his children, his grandchildren keep fond memories of him. One of his granddaughters wrote in *Valley East* 1850–2002:

> He was a wonderful man. He made us beautiful rocking chairs and rocking horses. My brother, Germain, and I would go to the river in the 4th concession and help him get beaver out of his traps. We would stay overnight in a little cabin by the river and sleep on mattresses. I remember when he made maple syrup. He was a real artist at carving wood.[21]

And What of the Future?

So Marie-Louise is growing up in a family dominated by a proud, active and enterprising father. As she is the oldest, the more her mother's health deteriorates, the less leisure time she has. In one interview, Marie-Louise's daughter Gertrude says to me:

> You know, at home [*in Hanmer*], before all the events, her sister Dorilla was disabled. She had had polio. And anyway, ... I imagine ... that my mother had to take care of her, too. Those were more responsibilities that she had. ... And I think that it must have been a pretty sad life ... Just work, work, work.[22]

Chairs made by Napoléon Labelle

At times, Marie-Louise must yearn to escape from all this drudgery. What does she see on the horizon when she thinks about her future? To grow up under Napoléon's rule doing hard domestic chores, only to get married and do the same thing for her husband and children in another little house in Hanmer? She can see no way out of the monotonous life awaiting her.

SPIRITUAL LIFE IN THE HAMLET

Hanmer continues to develop at a good pace. In 1906, the hamlet has a population of approximately 75 and counts a post office, a general store, a hotel, a sawmill and a blacksmith shop.[23] The hamlet's spiritual life is growing rapidly too. On the first Monday of every month, a missionary comes to say mass in a settler's home. But the settlers increasingly aspire to a continuous Church presence. Finally, in 1905 the Church decides to establish a parish and on 1 August 1906, Father Joseph A. Roy becomes the first parish priest in Hanmer.

CHAPTER TWO
1858 TO 1906
The New Arrival

His appearance in a home never failed to bring comfort, consolation and new hope. … He liked clean fun, … Wherever he went he left a ray of sunshine.

ᘐ ROMÉO BÉDARD,
Abbot. 1953. *History, Montmartre Sask.*
1893–1953, Regina Diocese, p. 6 & 7.

FATHER JOSEPH A. ROY

All his life, with few exceptions, he will sign his name "J.A. Roy," which would create some confusion in my research since in some documents referring to him I would find written in long form "Jérémie Alphonse Roy" and in others "Joseph Alphonse Roy." All the historical sources I consulted indicate that this is one and the same man. According to his baptismal certificate, he was born "Désiré Jérémie Roy." Désiré was his godfather's name. Later, I would be surprised to discover that he had made other creative alterations to his name and that the cloth of ambiguity surrounding his identity was only a reflection of the deeper ambiguity governing his beliefs, his actions and his emotions.

Upon his arrival in Hanmer in August 1906, Father Roy is 48 years old. At first sight, his cassock doesn't give anyone to suspect the pioneer life that he had led before coming to Hanmer. Born in 1858 on a farm in Berthierville, Quebec, he chose to leave farming and the family homestead behind to undertake classical studies at the Seminary in Joliette. He then entered the Grand Séminaire in Montreal, where he studied theology. He was ordained as a priest by Bishop Monsignor Fabre on 26 February 1888.[1] Afterwards, he would have become the vicar of Saint Eustache or of Saint-Valentin Parish near Montreal, a position he would have occupied for approximately two years (1888–1889).

THE FRANCOPHONE CATHOLIC CLERGY IN THE CANADIAN WEST

Father Jérémie becomes a priest during a bustling period in the history of the Catholic Church. Indeed, since 1870 the Catholic Church has given itself the mission to establish a French-Catholic presence on the entire Canadian territory. In the West, Monsignor Alexandre Taché, Bishop of Saint Boniface since 1854, works assiduously to ensure the rights of French Canadians and of the

Métis. In 1869, the Canadian government acquires Rupert's Land from the Hudson's Bay Company, setting off, as a domino effect, the Red River Rebellion (1869–1870). Feeling threatened by this acquisition, the Métis create a provisional government under the leadership of Louis Riel. The francophone Catholic clergy, sympathetic to the Métis cause, helps the provisional government to draft a list of Métis rights. Monsignor Taché, who lived for more than twenty years among the Métis, understands their concerns and tries to sensitize the Canadian government representatives but to no avail. Nevertheless, negotiations between Riel's provisional government and Canada come to a conclusion and, on 12 May 1870, Manitoba becomes the Canadian Confederation's fifth province. However, the Canadian government having refused to grant him amnesty, Riel is forced into exile in the United States.

Monsignor Taché, still convinced of the importance of increasing the French-speaking population in the West, launches a campaign to entice francophone settlers to the Northwest Territories. Missionary-colonizers travel throughout the province of Quebec extolling to would-be settlers the richness of the lands in the Prairies. Afterwards, they go to New England to convince French Canadians who had emigrated there to also come settle in the Northwest Territories.

Meanwhile, many settlers arrive in Saskatchewan. Some Métis who had moved there following the Red River Rebellion find themselves once more threatened with losing their lands. In 1884, they call Riel back from exile and once again form a provisional government. A new rebellion, the North West Rebellion (or Saskatchewan Rebellion) erupts in 1885. However, this time the Catholic Church steers clear of the Métis. After many bloody battles, the latter are defeated. Monsignor Taché pleads with the Canadian government to pardon Riel but in vain. On 16 November 1885, Riel is hanged in Regina.

The western francophone clergy's campaign to recruit French-speaking settlers keeps on spreading. Between 1885 and 1893, representatives from the Canadian government, including Father Antoine Labelle, go on a formal mission to French-speaking countries in Europe to promote the coming of francophone settlers to Canada. Pierre Foursin, Secretary to the Canadian High Commission in France, travels to Canada repeatedly to study the feasibility of such a project. Subsequently, he creates in Paris the Real Property Society of Canada, which finances sending francophone Catholic settlers to western Canada.

As early as 1887, the Church begins recruiting young francophone priests willing to open new missions in the West for the anticipated settlers. The adventure seems to have tempted young Father Jérémie since he accepts to become a missionary in the West in 1890.

WOLSELEY, SASKATCHEWAN

When Father Roy arrives as a vicar in Regina in 1890, the memory of Louis Riel's hanging in this city only five years before is still fresh in people's minds. The population in this territory, which will become Saskatchewan in 1905, is in full expansion. Between 1880 and 1911, it grows from 20,000 to 492,000 inhabitants. As for the number of farms, they increase from 1,500 in 1886 to 56,000 in 1906.[2]

Since Saint-Boniface in Manitoba is the only Episcopal seat in western Canada, few priests have yet taken up a ministry in the region. Therefore, each priest is entrusted with the responsibility for several missions. Soon after his arrival, Father Roy becomes the first resident pastor in Wolseley, situated 65 miles (105 km) east of Regina. During this ministry, his duties require him to travel constantly. The registers for Saint Anne's Parish reveal that Father Jérémie has under his purview, in addition to Wolseley, the missions situated in a 30- to 40-mile (48- to 64-km) radius around Wolseley: Qu'Appelle and Balgonie in the west, and in the east Grenfell, Broadview, and even Whitewood 46 miles (74 km) from

Wolseley. In addition, when the Montmartre mission is created in 1893, 47 miles (76 km) south of Wolseley, it also becomes his responsibility. Since these parishes are connected by dirt roads and the means of transportation in this era generally come down to a one-horse buggy, one can begin to grasp the breadth of Father Roy's responsibilities as he must regularly visit each parish, summer and winter alike, while making sure to be back in Wolseley every Sunday to say Mass.

Father J.A. Roy

On 20 March 1890, we find the first inscription under his name in the parish registers: the christening of a girl from Qu'Appelle. He signs, "J.A. Roy, priest." According to the 1928 version of the *Dictionnaire biographique du clergé canadien-français* (*the Dictionary of Biographies of French-Canadian Clergy*), the initials J.A. would stand for Jérémie Alphonse. But where does "Alphonse" come from, since it is not on his baptismal certificate? Is it a name adopted at the time of his ordination? That is a possibility. One should remember that since most people in this era were illiterate, excepting the clergy, names were adopted, used and spelled without following strict rules. They only become important when it came to signing official papers such as a baptismal certificate, a marriage license or a notarized document. Thus, it is quite possible that Jérémie had adopted Alphonse as a second name to use only from time to time, for example when signing official documents. In fact, the stories covering this period of his life seem to confirm this hypothesis since they indicate that people called him simply "Abbot Jérémie" or "Father Jérémie" or "Father Roy."

Research in the archives of the Saskatchewan Archives Board and of the Regina Archdiocese enable us to follow his trail and give us an idea of the tasks he accomplishes and the difficult conditions in which he works. The Wolseley presbytery where Father Roy lives intermittently between 1890 and 1900 consists only of two rooms: a bedroom and one other unadorned room serving as kitchen and dining room. A stove, a box for firewood, chairs, a table, and a storage chest for provisions constitute all the furniture in this room. As is the custom, the village curate gets room and board from the parishioners. They are responsible each in turn to keep his larder full. However, try as they may, it sometimes happens that the priest finds his chest empty if he comes home earlier than expected.

On 7 September 1890, we find him baptizing two children in Balgonie. On 14 November 1893, he makes a special trip to Montmartre to baptize the Simonins' daughter. In December of that same year, a Montmartre resident comes and fetches him in a hurry to administer the last rites to a Montmartre man suffering from pneumonia. Unfortunately, after having travelled 47 miles (76 kilometres) in the cold from Wolseley to Montmartre, the two men arrive too late: the patient has uttered his last breath. Father Roy sings a requiem mass for the deceased.[3]

The Roy Cross, erected by the citizens of Montmartre, Saskatchewan
(Courtesy of the Regina Archdiocese)

Father Roy maintains excellent relations with the Montmartre parishioners. They trust him and his presence comforts them in times of need. His sense of humour livens up every visit to Montmartre homes. It is not surprising therefore that the parishioners invite him to participate in important community events. For instance, on 1 April 1894, residents of Montmartre celebrate the first day of their first spring in Montmartre. They invite Father Roy to partake in their celebrations. He hears confession and sings a High Mass. This day will be remembered as a milestone in the history of Montmartre and the parishioners will be forever grateful to Father Roy, who accepted to come and share with them this historic moment. In 1926, they erect in Montmartre the Roy Cross to commemorate this important day.

Father Roy's tasks are not limited to administering the blessed sacraments or to saying mass for his flock. A letter dated July 1895 by a certain Martelle from Wolseley and addressed to Archbishop Langevin indicates that Father Roy also gave advice to some couples experiencing marital problems and that some of them separated after receiving his advice. The letter also refers to his taking care of many civil matters without describing their nature.[4] Mr. Martelle complains that Father Roy spends more time on these civil matters than on his religious tasks. His activities are not unanimously accepted by Wolseley parishioners, even though Father Roy is merely doing the duties expected of a parish priest of his day. *The priest was the driving force in a parish. Much respected, he could play the role of pedagogical, economic, legal and cultural advisor. The vitality of a parish was directly linked to the personality and energy of its curate.*[5] However, Father Roy does not always share his superior's views on questions of morality. He understands and shares the settlers' life and the harsh conditions in which they live, with the result that he indulges them and lets them enjoy the small pleasures their rustic life affords them. But his Archbishop in Saint-Boniface does not see things that way. Thus Father Roy finds himself sometimes between a rock and a hard place, as evidenced by the visit he reluctantly makes to Montmartre at the beginning of the year in 1896:

> In fact at the beginning of the year 1896, in one of his rare visits to Montmartre, the pastor of Wolseley had come to announce to Mr. and Mrs. De Tremaudan that he had received orders to have these evenings of dancing stopped. The good priest admitted that, personally, he understood that the dances at Montmartre were well conducted, but he still was obliged to carry out the instructions received. The clergy of Canada would not tolerate dancing, especially dances

such as the waltz, the polka, the mazurka, and it even went so far as to refuse the sacraments to persons who participated or organized dances. The pastor also advised that the young folks of Wolseley be no longer invited to any reunion whatsoever; the French Canadian parents complained that the young folks were not able to work the next day after passing the night dancing at Montmartre.[6]

The correspondence that Father Roy entertained with his Archbishop, Monsignor Langevin, between 1896 and 1900, reveals a man tired of the physical and moral sacrifices inherent in his life as a priest/missionary. At the instigation of Monsignor Langevin, he undertakes the construction of the Wolseley church but does it reluctantly, as evidenced in his 24 March 1896 letter to the Archbishop:

> *"Truthfully, my parishioners do not deserve the sacrifices and risks that we impose on ourselves. I find myself getting disgusted and I am tempted to abandon them and to take off elsewhere. I will start this construction but I do not promise to complete it. Pray for me, Monsignor ..."*

This construction causes him unrelenting financial worries and multiple arguments with the parishioners' committee involved in the project. How he would like to escape from this burden! On numerous occasions, he asks Monsignor Langevin to assign him to a ministry elsewhere. He suggests the Klondike or the West. Finally, in early 1900, the ecclesiastic authorities send him to Vernon, British Columbia. The last inscription under his name in the Wolseley parish registry is dated 12 April 1900. It is for the baptism of a boy, son of a farmer named Gérald Seymour from Sintaluta. The child inherits the first names Gérald Roy.

Saint Anne church built in Wolseley, Saskatchewan
under the supervision of J.A. Roy *(Courtesy of the Regina Archdiocese)*

The citizens of Montmartre feel a great deal of sadness to see him go. The portrait they write of him in the *History of Montmartre* attests to the warm human relationships he maintained with them:

> Gifted with a lively deeply-rooted faith, he devoted himself wholeheartedly to the temporal as well as the spiritual welfare of his flock, and shared their trials, tribulations and privations, which he himself had experienced. They placed all their confidence in him. His appearance in a home never failed to bring comfort, consolation and new hope. He settled quarrels and renewed their courage. He was indulgent towards sinners, but was a staunch enemy to sin himself under any of its forms. He roused the sluggish and encouraged the timid. He liked clean fun, and this was very necessary to the men of the prairies. Wherever he went, he left a ray of sunshine. Such was the Missionary-Pastor who was to exert a profound and lasting influence on the colonists of Montmartre, either by visits to their dwellings or by his ministry in the poor church at Wolseley.[7]

Father Roy is therefore assigned to St. James Parish in Vernon. His first inscription in the parish baptismal registry is dated 27 May 1900. I could not find any details regarding this period of his life in Vernon. I only know that in 1901 two of the "best families" from Wolseley moved there to join him because the climate is more pleasant.[8]

One could expect that this new ministry would free him from criticism by the parishioners' committee in Wolseley and put an end to his worries. Unfortunately, he continues to receive letters from Monsignor Langevin regarding Wolseley's financial problems. The tone of his replies indicates how exasperated he is with the petty complaints about him and how hurt he is by Monsignor Langevin's apparent lack of trust in him. The last three lines of his 2 May 1900 letter are a cry from his heart: *"Let me tell you, Monsignor, that if you want to discourage me you only have to keep up this pestering. I can readily give up my ministry. I can live without this."*[9]

Is it only frustration that makes him threaten to renounce the priesthood, or is he beginning to have doubts about his vocation? We can't tell. But he certainly harbours ambiguous feelings about his ministry.

The last inscription under his name in the baptismal registry in St James Parish is on 20 September 1905. Then I find no trace of him until a year later, in August 1906. What does Father Roy do during this period? Does he take a leave of absence to reflect on his future? Does he return to his family in the Province of Quebec to rest for a few months? We can surmise that he spends part of the time negotiating with the Church regarding the destination of his next assignment. But something definitely important occurs during this year because it is a "new" Father Roy who finds himself assigned to the hamlet of Hanmer, a small francophone enclave in northern Ontario where, in the late nineteenth century, economic development is mostly governed by anglophone masters.

HANMER, ONTARIO (AUGUST 1906)

On 1 August 1906, Father Roy takes up his duties as the first parish priest in Hanmer. He has not just donned new responsibilities: he seems to have also acquired a new identity during the past year. Indeed, during my interviews with Marie-Louise's family members in Hanmer, the issue of Father Roy's identity crops up when I refer to him as "Jérémie." His niece corrects me:

> His name is "Joseph." We never heard anything else besides Joseph. In all the books it was always "Joseph Roy," Joseph A. Roy. Joseph Alphonse, I believe.[10]

She is right! Later I discover documents from this period signed by Father Roy showing in his handwriting "Joseph A. Roy." I tell myself that he might have simply chosen to use Joseph instead of Jérémie. It is plausible because in this era all boys were christened with the first name of Joseph and all girls with the first name of Mary. This first name would be followed by two or more given names: Joseph François Aimé or Joseph Louis Victor or Joseph Napoléon, etc. But on his baptismal certificate I do not find Joseph. I pursue my research and consult once more the *Dictionnaire biographique du clergé canadien-français*. The 1908 and 1928 editions clearly indicate that Father J.A. Roy, missionary in western Canada, and Father Jérémie Alphonse Roy, first curate of Hanmer, are one and the same person. So why does he introduce himself to his parishioners as Joseph Alphonse instead of Jérémie Alphonse? Is he trying to cover up something in his past? What happened between Vernon and Hanmer? I never found the answers to these questions and they only increase the ambiguity clouding the portrait of this man.

Whatever the case may be, whether he presents himself as Jérémie or Joseph does not change the fact that he is ideally suited to establish a parish in Hanmer. His ministry in the West endowed him with all the experience he needs to take on the task. For him, it is only one more French Catholic mission to found in a land of colonization. His duties also cover the nearby township of Capreol. As in the West, he will have to travel around frequently with precarious means of transportation and in sometimes inclement weather. So he understands the challenges ahead of him! But what he cannot foresee upon his arrival is that he will discover during this mission another very agreeable side to life that will turn his beliefs upside down and provoke a tortuous emotional development in his heart of hearts.

FIRST MEETING WITH MARIE-LOUISE

As the parish's new curate, Joseph Roy's first duty is to make the rounds of the homes and introduce himself to the settlers. He shakes hands with the parents and says a few kind words to the children. At Napoléon Labelle's house, he meets Marie-Louise for the first time. She is 15 years old. They probably exchange a smile and a few pleasantries at the most.

He leaves a good impression in Hanmer homes and, the following year, he doesn't take long to fulfill the settlers' fondest dream, that of building the hamlet's first chapel.[11] This small chapel strengthens the community's identity. Hanmer is no longer just an agglomeration of settlers that receives a priest once a month when he comes to say mass. Hanmer is now a parish where a resident priest administers the sacraments and teaches catechism to the children. Christenings, weddings and first communions follow one another and ensure stability in the settlers' spiritual, emotional and social life.

CHAPTER THREE

1906 TO *1916*

The Turning Point

He felt that she was one of those women who, when they give themselves, give everything without counting: the love of their body and their heart, the strength of their arms in everyday tasks, the total devotion of a mind without artifice.

⌐ LOUIS HÉMON,
Maria Chapdelaine, Editions Fides,
pages 88 and 89

Father Roy maintains close ties with the families in Hanmer through his regular parish visits. But he seems to maintain a closer tie with the Labelle family since in the years following his arrival in Hanmer he bought five lots in the Hanmer and Capreol counties, making him one of the most important landowners in the township.[1] And it so happens that from 1911 to 1913 Napoléon Labelle, Marie-Louise's father, is one of Hanmer's four local councillors and it is the local council that normally holds the register of the township land sales and purchases.

Thus Father Roy goes to the Labelle's home to discuss the necessary land transactions with Napoléon, and also to chat with him about this and that. The two men have a lot in common. They have both known pioneer life and share some personality traits. Fiercely independent, they both like to be master of their own decisions and they are both gifted in organizing communities. But their tempers differ greatly: Napoléon is impetuous, and Joseph is gentle. Napoléon expresses himself with a fiery discourse whereas Joseph has learned the art of listening.

It is surely during these visits that Father Roy and Marie-Louise discover the undeniable pleasure of seeing and talking with one another. The priest appreciates Marie-Louise's quick wit and her playful banter. He is sensitive to the admiration she feels for him and that she can't dissemble. Moreover, Marie-Louise is turning into a beautiful woman. The family photo taken around 1908 and reprinted in *Valley East* reveals a young woman of about 17 or 18 dressed in a lace blouse with a high collar and a long skirt. She has put up her hair in a chignon. Her beautiful forehead thus freed accentuates the oval of her face. Her big eyes reflect a patient expression. But her shapely lips hardly show a shadow of a smile and betray a firm inner determination. Just as the great river near which she first saw light, she gives an impression of calm inner strength and, like that water, she possesses a powerful underlying current that can sweep everything away.

The Labelle family: Marie-Louise is to the right of her adoptive father
Napoléon. Georgianne, Marie-Louise's mother, is standing. Circa 1907.
(Courtesy of the Greater Sudbury Library)

In 1912, Father Roy is 54 years old. He has spent most of his life in
the rough environment of the colonies. Since he has hardly known
the comforts of urban presbyteries, he probably appreciates the gen-
tility of evenings spent at the Labelle's, where Marie-Louise serves
him tea and sweets accompanied by a smile and a nice word. When
I met Marie-Louise's niece in Hanmer, she had the same interpretation of the facts:

> *... That is MY vision of her, not my mother's vision.*
> *... He arrives in 1906, and there were probably 20*
> *to 30 farmers. These were large families. They lived*
> *miserable lives, in terrible conditions, and houses that*
> *weren't very good. And he had a house. He needed*
> *someone. And, all of a sudden, this young girl ar-*
> *rives, she is a little delicate, she likes nice things. And*
> *for him, it is like a breath of fresh air arriving in the*

midst of all these farmers. ... And I know that my
aunt loved to drink tea. And I can almost see her ...
when she served the priest his tea: "Come, sit down,
have a cup of tea." With all of her gentleness. That is
my version.[2]

The priest's visits amuse Marie-Louise. They say he liked to talk
about his adventures out West. His stories open a window on a
whole new world that gives the young woman the desire to travel.
She would love to explore new places. She begins to realize to what
extent she is confined in this little house, harnessed to the routine
of daily chores. Her only outings are the visits to church on Sun-
days. Because she was entrusted with many responsibilities since
her childhood, she is very mature for a young woman of her age.
It is therefore not surprising that she can develop a friendship with
Father Roy, even though he is thirty-three years her senior.

PRESBYTERY MAID?

How did Marie-Louise end up becoming the maid in Hanmer's
presbytery around 1912? Only knowledge of the mentality and
conventions of the day allow me to infer the unfolding of events.
The priest and Marie-Louise feel, without admitting it, an increasing desire to see each other more often. The abbot rationalizes his
inclination by telling himself that he would really need help with
the presbytery. Marie-Louise would be an ideal candidate for the
job. He knows her well; he has seen in what impeccable manner
she keeps house and has tasted her cooking during his visits to the
Labelle household. Custom would warrant that he first ask Napoléon and Georgianne if their daughter could come work days
at the presbytery. Marie-Louise's parents would never consider re-
fusing such a service to the parish priest. On the contrary! It is an
honour for them that he chooses to entrust their daughter with

the responsibility of taking care of his home. And besides, Claire, Marie-Louise's little sister, has grown up and can take on many of the routine chores. They consult Marie-Louise, who accepts with deference, all the while repressing an outburst of secret joy.

An unmarried 21-year-old woman working for a member of the clergy could cause tongues to wag. Since the late sixteenth century in Europe, tradition would have it that priests hire as servants only women in their thirties or forties, in order to avoid "temptations" and to prevent gossip in prudish society.[3] French Canada in the early twentieth century preserves this tradition. A woman who wishes to work in a presbytery *"must, to be hired, be advanced in years (40 years old), not lend herself to unfavourable gossip, and not allow in the least that the priest's reputation be put into question because of her presence."*[4] But circumstances sometimes dictate exceptions to this rule. Marie-Louise's reputation is without blemish and her talents as a homemaker are well known and justify her selection. And the folks in Hanmer are aware that the Father knows Napoléon very well. Marie-Louise's presence in the presbytery thus does not endanger the priest's reputation.

Details of the inception of their secret love life went to the grave with them. One can only imagine how their passion saw the light of day. Marie-Louise and Joseph are happy to be working side by side. For her, it is a change of scenery and a variation in her daily tasks. For him, it is a feminine presence by his side, an expert hand to care for his house and a discreet individual to whom he can confide certain thoughts. At first, they do their best to speak only of topics concerning the presbytery maintenance. But soon, as with all individuals who see each other regularly, they come to share impressions, memories and dreams. The days and months pass, bringing them closer and closer. They laugh together, but their laugh now betrays a feverish love that they struggle to contain.

The historical documents that I consulted indicated that Father J.A. Roy served in Saint Jacques' Parish in Hanmer until

29 September 1913, and that he was then assigned to Cache Bay on the shores of Lake Nipissing sixty miles (100 kilometres) from Hanmer. Cache Bay was a small, mainly francophone town on the outskirts of Sturgeon Falls. When Father Roy arrives, its economy depends mostly on the prosperity of the sawmill, George Gordon Lumber, which milled the logs floated down the Sturgeon River.

I was unable to find data about Marie-Louise and Joseph's relations between October 1913 and April 1917. But the events that enfolded demonstrate that Father Roy's transfer to Cache Bay did not end their relationship, and allow us to infer the nature of their bond. Since they worked side by side for the entire previous year, Marie-Louise feels a lot of sadness to see him move away from Hanmer. Furthermore, his departure implies that she will have to return to the drudgery of housework, confined to her father's home. For his part, Joseph might not mind serving in a new parish but he is unhappy about leaving Marie-Louise. It does not take him long to come up with a plan for seeing her on a regular basis. Using as a pretext that he will need help to set up and maintain order in the Cache Bay presbytery, he asks Marie-Louise's parents if they would mind her coming by train to Cache Bay from time to time to give him a hand. Since 1883, the Canadian Pacific serves cities between North Bay and Sudbury. Napoléon could bring her to the Sudbury station and Father Roy would pick her up at the Sturgeon Falls station. However, since the train does not run daily, this new arrangement would require that Marie-Louise sleep over in Cache Bay for a night or two. But Napoléon and Georgianne would never question the good intentions of this priest whom they have known for seven years and received frequently in their home.

Marie-Louise and Joseph's periodic co-habitation in the Cache Bay presbytery only serves to exacerbate the love fever that they felt in Hanmer. Here they find themselves in a new presbytery, far from the proper supervision of Marie-Louise's family and of the people of Hanmer. Marie-Louise's short stays probably go unnoticed by the parishioners of Cache Bay. Father Roy conducts his ministry in church while Marie-Louise works discretely to make the new presbytery comfortable. In the evening, they share an intimate diner. The long nights of dialoguing stretch out and soon their desire conquers all: doubts, social conventions and religious convictions.

In reality, what transpires in their hearts may be less simple and romantic than I like to imagine. Joseph undoubtedly feels mixed emotions, a secret battle between his religious convictions and the inescapable rise of the physical desire that gets the better of him and to which he surrenders with delight. Gertrude, Marie-Louise's daughter, is more realistic than I am. With the humour and the wisdom of a mature woman, she tells me, *"His mid-life crisis got him."*[5]

And it is certainly true! Joseph is probably very confused by the intense happiness that he feels. Does he really not have the makings of a priest after all? He would have chosen the wrong vocation since he feels no regrets. He can't believe that such a shared happiness could be a sin.

As for Marie-Louise, the fact that this educated, mature man loves her fills her with joy and pride. She would like to shout it from the rooftops and show their love to everyone in the community. But she stays silent and resolutely hides her happiness to preserve her chances of seeing her fondest dream materialize, her dream of one day living openly with him. She can imagine their life as a couple in a city where, incognito, they would go about their affairs without fear of gossip. Hanmer is stifling her! During all her childhood years, she has seen the women around her harnessed to their daily tasks with the only recognition that of being called "Queen of the household" by their husbands or by the priest in his sermons. She does not want such a thankless, dead-end future. She wants to get out of her hamlet. She wants to live elsewhere and especially elsewhere with Joseph.

Marie-Louise around the time she fell in love

AGAINST ALL COMERS

In spite of the strong emotions clawing at their heart, their love strengthens with the passing days. The illicit nature of their relationship only brings them closer together. They are well aware of contravening all social and religious codes of conduct. In this era, a woman who took the liberty of having sexual relations outside of marriage came in for social reproof. In this instance, it is additionally with a priest, and a priest who is thirty-three years older than her at that! It would be a monumental scandal if the affair would be found out! Thus, Marie-Louise and Joseph hide their love like happy children acting in collusion.

Do they take precautions to avoid Marie-Louise getting pregnant? What does she know about sexuality and birth control? Probably very little. Between 1869 and 1916, works have been published recommending "periodic abstention"[6] but Marie-Louise can hardly read or write. Besides, most of these publications are in English. There is one manual about sexuality written by a French doctor, Dr. Auguste de Bey, but *the Church makes every effort to keep information about sexuality and contraception far away for the faithful.*[7] Thus it is highly improbable that these publications were circulating in Hanmer. As for Joseph, he surely knows more than her in these matters. But since sexuality is a taboo subject in those days, he may not feel comfortable talking openly about it with her, even in intimate moments. What's more, his religious education always taught him that sex is only acceptable if its goal is procreation. This precept might even hold him back from curbing his lovemaking and incline him instead to simply let nature run its course. It is also possible that physical pleasure temporarily hides from his mind the consequences that the arrival of a child could have.

The fact remains that, in August 1916, Marie-Louise, who is still living with her parents in Hanmer, discovers that she is pregnant. She is fraught with questions. Who can she turn to? Should she confide this terrible secret to her parents? Will they renounce her forever? Will they become the shame of Hanmer? And what will her lover say? She decides not to tell her parents right away for fear that they will not let her return to Cache Bay. She anxiously awaits her next trip while imagining all kinds of scenarios in which she announces to Joseph that he is about to become a father.

No doubt, the news arouses a surge of thoughts and emotions in this 58-year-old priest. He has never known a life other than that of a man of the cloth. At the same time, he does not doubt his love for Marie-Louise. Until now, he has managed to devote himself to both the Church and his love. But now the imminent arrival of this child forces him to choose between the two. The new emotion of knowing he will be a father and the deep sense of responsibility that he feels towards this young 25-year-old woman soon stifle any doubts he might have felt at the thought of leaving his ministry. He takes action.

FLIGHT

Marie-Louise's pregnancy and the enormity of the scandal it would cause if their affair should be discovered explain why they escape from Cache Bay without Joseph requesting a dispensation from the Catholic Church. Historical documents lead one to believe that Joseph had for some time contemplated leaving the priesthood, for he had begun in 1911 to resell some of the land he had bought during his early years in Hanmer. When one examines carefully the legal documents of purchases and sales of his lands, one notices that on the purchase documents, he was identified as "Joseph A. Roy, Catholic priest." Yet, on the sales documents of 15 April 1911 and of 19 May 1913, after Marie-Louise had begun working for him at the presbytery, he is identified as "Joseph A. Roy, an unmarried man." I would be unable to determine if this choice of words is that of Father Roy or of the notary who drew up the papers but they reflect, voluntarily or not, a change in Father Roy's status.

IMPACT OF THEIR DEPARTURE

When I inquire in Hanmer about the impact of the lovers' departure, the answers I receive mention only the repercussions on the family. Marie-Louise's niece tells me, *"Napoléon was furious and hurt."* And she adds, *"They say he was so angry that he wanted to go down to Ottawa and kill him."* [8]

Marie-Louise's other niece confirms this story:

> *And he went to Ottawa with a gun to kill him but*
> *he never found him. ... My mother told me that and*
> *said, "I always thanked God that he never found him,*
> *because he had brought a gun with him."* [9]

Fact or fiction? Knowing Napoléon's fiery temper, such a story seems plausible but we have no way to verify its truthfulness.

One thing is sure: Napoléon loves his daughter and, as Gertrude confirms to me, this departure afflicts him terribly.

> *He was very upset and her mother felt a deep sadness*
> *that affected her naturally. And besides, they relied so*
> *much on her to take care of the house, you know, and*
> *of the young children, her sisters and brothers. So I can*
> *understand that he was very angry.* [10]

Georgianne, like any mother who sees her daughter leave, undoubtedly experiences mixed emotions about her daughter's love escapade. On one hand, she can understand her husband's anger because he feels so betrayed by Father Roy whom he had treated like a friend. But on the other hand, she is secretly delighted at Marie-Louise's happiness. Good for her if she can escape this life of exhausting labour and the stifling mentality of this small village where everyone spies and gossips on the life of everyone else! More power to her if she can live a romantic love instead of simply accepting to marry for practical reasons. May God bless her!

During my interviews in Hanmer, no one mentions that a scandal occurred in the village after Marie-Louise's departure. I deduce from this that Napoléon and Georgianne probably did everything in their power to avoid the story being spread. Fearing to lose face in Hanmer, they would have explained Marie-Louise's absence by saying that she had found work in Ottawa.

But Napoléon finds himself in a very delicate situation in the community because, at the time of the lovers' departure, he is still one of the four municipal councillors in Hanmer. Upon careful examination of documents in the archives, I notice that the following year his name does not appear anymore on the list of councillors. Maybe it is simply because his term is over. After all, he has been holding this function since 1911. But it may also be because he prefers to leave this position, to keep a lower profile in the community. This way, he can avoid meetings during which he could be asked friendly questions about his daughter.

CHAPTER FOUR

1916 to 1928

Family Life

We had a quiet family life there.

From recording prepared by
ℰ GERTRUDE MANTHA,
November 2004–March 2005

NEW IDENTITIES

Upon leaving Cache Bay, the lovers take refuge in Ottawa, the individualistic nature of life in cities making it easier to hide their love. They adopt new identities. Joseph anglicizes his family name: the francophone Joseph Roy becomes the anglophone Joseph Ray and Marie-Louise Labelle introduces herself from now on as Marie-Louise Ray. I wonder if when they change their names Joseph reveals to Marie-Louise that he was baptized Désiré Jérémie and that he was known as Jérémie Alphonse during his stay out West. Maybe not. After all, she has only known him as Joseph A. Roy.

Marie-Louise surely hopes that Joseph will marry her. Living in a common law relationship is not socially admissible in those days. In leaving Hanmer, her parents, brothers and sisters, she gave up everything for him, including her reputation. But Joseph chooses an ambiguous position. On the one hand, he has rejected the Church in leaving it without asking for a dispensation. On the other hand, he refrains from turning his back on the Church completely by marrying Marie-Louise, since if he were to do so he would be excommunicated. For a man of the cloth, being excommunicated is unthinkable. So he chooses instead to not break definitely with the Church and to not commit himself permanently to Marie-Louise. After all, it is easier to live in ambiguity than to commit to a definite choice. Easy for him. More difficult for Marie-Louise.

OTTAWA

Moving from Hanmer to Ottawa constitutes a major step in Marie-Louise's life. Hanmer had only about one hundred inhabitants whereas Ottawa in 1916 has a population of 100,561. In contrast with the homogeneous francophone and Catholic population of Hanmer, Ottawa distinguishes itself by its cultural diversity. Irish and French-Catholics mix with Jews, Germans and Italians. When Joseph and Marie-Louise arrive in the capital, the war in Europe is breathing new life into the country's economy. Ottawa is undergoing a transformation passing gradually from an economy dependent on the forest industry to an economy based on the growth of the civil service. On Parliament Hill, work is in progress to reconstruct Parliament's Centre Block, destroyed in a fire on February 3rd that same year. Grand houses are starting to go up in the Glebe, on Clemow Avenue among other streets.[1] Lansdowne Park is home to summer and winter sporting activities and to the annual agricultural and industrial fair in the fall.[2]

It is the first time that Marie-Louise lives in a city and everything represents novelty and learning. She must get her bearings, distinguish "upper town" from "lower town," and travel through them on a streetcar. Around her, women have gradually started to join the labour market as men are marching off to war. Women are discovering the advantages of earning a salary and are gaining a taste for independence. Many of them have a "career" in the service industries, particularly as domestic help, before getting married.

Marie-Louise discovers the abundance of department stores with the latest in feminine fashions, material by the yards as well as ready-made clothes. On sunny days, she and Joseph can stroll along the canal where high society ladies ride their horses down the Driveway lined with hundred-year-old trees. Every day brings something new and, for this newly arrived couple, the general environment of growth and expansion inspires them to make plans for the future.

RIDEAU PARK (MAY 1917)

While awaiting the baby's birth, Marie-Louise and Joseph look for a good place to bring up their child. They want a location where they can have a garden, raise some animals, and sell the fruits of their labour. They need money. Joseph has subdivided into two lots one of the parcels of land that he had bought in the township of Capreol in September 1911. On 3 January 1917 he sells one of them for $2,000.

On 12 April 1917, Marie-Louise gives birth to a son. For any woman in love with her partner, such an event is a source of great joy and pride. All the more so for Marie-Louise, as this birth marks an important milestone in her relationship with Joseph. They are no longer merely lovers. They are now parents. For Marie-Louise, this child represents the foundation of a new family that will fill the void left by the absence of the members of her family who are no longer part of her daily life. Joseph baptizes the child himself. They choose to call him Joseph Ray. An influenza epidemic is raging in the Capital and Marie-Louise undoubtedly takes extra precaution to protect her newborn child from this threat.

A month later, on 21 May 1917, Joseph buys in Rideau Park for the amount of $5,000 a house with 2 acres of land, including a barn and an apple orchard. The deed of sale stipulates that it is Lots 133, 134 and 135 facing Stanley Avenue (today known as Pleasant Park Avenue) as well as Lots 187, 188 and 189 facing Billings Avenue. The new owner signs simply "Joseph Ray," his own name and also that of his newborn son. Rideau Park is a small neighbourhood with wooden sidewalks, where a few French-speaking families live among a majority of anglophone families. It is located on the south side of the Rideau River near the train tracks, slightly removed from the "village" of Billings Bridge. The church, post office and stores in the village serve the inhabitants of Rideau Park and its surroundings.

Joseph and Marie-Louise have chosen a house that measures up to their dreams, a rather spacious house that would allow them to eventually raise a larger family. In addition to the living room, dining room and three bedrooms, a large summer kitchen makes it easier to make cider, to prepare butter, cheese, preserves, and slow-cooked meals, and to butcher provisions in the fall. When snow arrives, they close the summer kitchen and use the dining room as the winter kitchen. Although unfinished, the basement serves for storage, and a hole in the floor hides a freshwater spring where Joseph and Marie-Louise keep milk, butter and other supplies cool. In the front of the house, a large porch with vine-covered pillars invites one to rest.[3] This unpretentious home will witness the happiest and the worse moments of Marie-Louise's life.

Today, 279 Pleasant Park (formerly Stanley Street), in Rideau Park

LIFE AS A COUPLE

We had a quiet family life there.[4]

A family life! Marie-Louise's dream has become reality. She lives with the man she loves in their own home with their newborn child. They are happy.

> *They got along well. They did not squabble. … They sang a lot. They sang folk songs. Yes, I remember that. I believe that they really got along well because I can't*

remember any arguments. And, they had to love each
other very much to have gone through all that. … It
was true love.[5]

During the winter of 1918, Marie-Louise is once again pregnant. But the couple's joy is tainted with fear because a terrible Spanish flu epidemic just hit Ottawa. It lasts all winter. City authorities take extreme measures to check the disease, but it will only abate in the spring of 1919. Thanks to countless precautions taken by Joseph and Marie-Louise, the epidemic does not infiltrate the little home on Stanley Ave.

Joseph, far-sighted, takes the necessary financial steps to care for his growing family. On 23 August 1918, he sells for $900 the second part of the lot that he had bought in the township of Capreol in September 1911 and had subsequently subdivided.

A few months later, on 30 October 1918, the day Joseph turns 60, Marie-Louise gives birth to a daughter in a small, private hospital located at 183–185 Somerset Street West, on the corner of Elgin Street. What a birthday gift! They now have a boy and a girl. This birth fulfills their happiness. As he had done for their son, Joseph baptizes the baby himself. Bent over the tiny face, how moved he must be to pour Holy water on his own child's head! He must perform this ritual with all the love and tenderness that a father's heart can hold. They name their daughter Gertrude Ray. Does the arrival of this new little life make Joseph feel younger or older? Perhaps he feels more intensely the difference in age separating him from Marie-Louise. She is merely 27 years old and probably only sees the bright side of this new addition: the joy of having a girl, an additional bond with the man she loves, and the pleasure of having given him this child on his birthday. As for him, he sees slipping away the time when he and Marie-Louise were alone to enjoy the simple pleasures of life. This child reminds him in a very concrete way of their daily life's increasing responsibilities.

But such thoughts disappear like passing shadows when, less than 15 days later, on 11 November 1918, Germany signs the Armistice. The news spreads in the streets and houses like a warm southern breeze easing pains and soothing hearts. The war is over, to everyone's joy!

DAILY LIFE

As with most semi-rural families of their day, Marie-Louise and Joseph raise a few animals, cultivate a patch of land and earn an income by selling their produce. They have known country living and have all the experience necessary. They own a horse named Carney, and a cow. They sell milk to people like their neighbours, the Christies and the Laings. In addition to housekeeping, Marie-Louise separates the cream from the milk and churns it into butter. She also makes cottage cheese in her summer kitchen. Gertrude remembers her mother's sewing:

> *She sewed all our clothes [as well as] our winter coats. And for the boys she made, until they reached a certain age, their pants and everything. A lot of sewing, you know.*[6]

During my interviews with her, Gertrude comes back several times to her mother's exceptional talents as a seamstress.

> *She sewed BEAUTIFULLY really. … She made everything: coats, suits for the boys, and … There was nothing she couldn't do. And it was VERY well done.*[7]

Thus Marie-Louise's days are very full. Since there are no modern appliances in those days, each task requires a lot of time and effort.

In those days, there were no conveniences. So laundry was quite an affair! They had what they called "duffle boards," you know, and large tubs. Those must have contained approximately four huge pails of water. And you boiled your white linens in that to make them whiter. And naturally there were no driers either. So you had to hang it all up on the clothesline.[8]

Joseph is also very busy. He has over 100 chickens and has developed quite a clientele. Gertrude reminisces:

I got up with my father sometimes at 5 am because ... he had farm chores. So I often had breakfast with him. ... He sold eggs. He had clients in the Glebe, I remember that.[9] [She laughs as she looks at me, because I live in the Glebe.] *And [his clients] gave him the crusts that they cut from their sandwiches, you know. So he made us French toast with those crusts. That's what we had for breakfast. And I, I liked being alone with him because I guess he talked with me, and, I don't know. And Mother slept a little longer.*[10]

Marie-Louise and Joseph also grow a rather large garden.

C: *Did your father grow tobacco in his garden?*
G: *I think so because he smoked a pipe.*
C: *What else did he grow in the garden?*
G: *Well it was a fairly big garden. In those days, everybody had a garden. All the vegetables for the winter, you know. It was all there.*
C: *Carrots, peas, beans, and all that?*
G: *Yes.*
C: *Was it your mother who managed the garden?*

G: *Mostly.*
C: *And him? Did he grow his tobacco himself?*
G: *Well, I guess he was working in the garden too, you know.*
C: *They helped each other.*[11]

The garden's constant guardian is named Fairy. He is the family dog, a mutt with a personality like no other who took upon himself the task of chasing out mercilessly the chickens that venture into the garden.

G: *We sent the dog. We would say, "Fairy! Chickens in the garden!" and he chased them out of the garden. But you know most of the time, they were not loose, they were in a hen house.*[12]

When Gertrude's brother, Lorne, comes back to this story, I ask him:

C: Who trained him?
L: Oh, we didn't train him. He trained us![13]

The family eats healthy food. With produce from the garden, Marie-Louise cans preserves for the winter. She and Joseph know how to make the best of seasonal offerings.

G: *They were interested in eating well. We ate dandelions, you know, when they were in season.*
C: *Yes, the leaves.*
G: *They were like spinach.*
C: *Yes. Yes. We still eat them today. They put them more and more in salad mixes because they are good for one's health.*
G: *Yes, that's right.*[14]

So the children grow up in good health, with fresh air and natural produce. Although Marie-Louise and Joseph help each other and share daily chores, there is no doubt that Joseph remains the undisputable head of the household. He manages the property, watches over expenses, makes any large purchases for the household and deals with the clients. It is the family model that Marie-Louise is used to. Her adoptive father, Napoléon, earned the family's living. Since her domestic tasks keep her busy every waking hour, she no doubt appreciates having someone nearby on whom she can count to manage the finances.

Joseph loves his children. He takes his role as father to heart and participates in their education. Gertrude still has fond memories about those days with her father.

> G: *I remember sitting on his lap and he would sing to me.*
> C: *Oh yes? What kind of songs?*
> G: *Songs like 'La Poule grise" and things like that. … And I remember combing his hair. And he had beautiful, wavy hair. So I would comb it in funny styles, to make him laugh. No, I have good memories of him like that.*[15]

But Joseph can also be very hard on the children when they behave irresponsibly. The daughter of Marie-Louise and Joseph's eldest son, Joe, told me a story that happened to her Dad:

> My dad was terrible, a rascal, he would get in trouble sometimes. He went for a ride on a horse with another kid. They had horses. And had a great time! A big long hard ride and came back and put the horse in the barn and came in. … And his dad whipped him for that because what he did was

he left that animal sweating in the barn and he could have died. … He was so angry at the careless, thoughtless thing that my dad had done by leaving that animal and not even thinking.[16]

It is true that Joe is full of mischief, like most boys of his age, and that he deserves a scolding from time to time. In those days, it was acceptable to hit a child as punishment. Sometimes they used a leather belt or the leather shaving strap used to sharpen razor blades. Joe understands that he deserves to be reprimanded but he does not agree with the method. All his life, he will resent having been hit by his father.

INTELLECTUAL LIFE

Joseph had a classical education. He recognizes the importance of a formal education and cares about his children's intellectual development. He always keeps in mind the fact that Marie-Louise had very little chance to attend school and that her capacity to read and write remain very limited.

> **G:** *She had almost no education really. … She had learned to write a little, but she had difficulty spelling. … You know, she did not know grammar.*
> **C:** *When she lived with him, after you were born, did she continue to learn reading and writing with him?*
> **G:** *I imagine that he may have helped her. It's possible, yes, because he read a lot. I remember that he would go to the Carnegie Library. Every year they would sell books; they would recycle books. He would arrive with boxes of books. I imagine that she must taken advantage of these books.[17] There were always books in our house.[18]*

One of these books is among the souvenirs that one of Marie-Louise's grandsons, Patrick, has kept from his grandparents. When I met him for the interview, he arrived with a book in hand.

> *I brought a book that supposedly belonged to my grandfather. ... My grandmother gave it to me.*

He hands me a book entitled *Les soirées du Château de Ramezay*, published by l'École littéraire de Montréal in 1900. It contains short stories, extracts of plays and mostly poems by Émile Nelligan and other poets.

> C: *So he liked poetry.*
> P: *Well, I guess so.*
> C: *What about her, did she read that? Was she literate enough to read it?*
> P: *I wouldn't think so.*[19]

It is quite possible that in the evening, once the children went to bed, Joseph and Marie-Louise, seated side by side, spend a few moments reading. Maybe he read to her, from this book, Nelligan's poem *"Immaculate Love,"* in which mystical love fuses with profane love in the poet's heart. As a priest, he might have been particularly attracted to this poem that starts with, *"I know a marvelous stained-glass window in a church."* He might have lovingly bent over her while reading to her with a smile, *"My romantic beloved, ... you, the only one I love and will always love."* And the last lines, would he have read them with a sombre foreboding in his heart?

> *You, who stay silent, impassive and proud,*
> *Perhaps you will see me, sombre and desperate,*
> *Wander in my love as in a cemetery.*[20]

SPIRITUAL LIFE

The Ray family lives the life of a typical Rideau Park family, except for one important difference: they keep their spiritual life private. They have cast aside weekly religious rituals. The family does not go to mass and does not pray at all as a family. Yet, they remain believers. Joseph insisted on baptizing his children and he wants them to take their First Communion and their Confirmation. He still thinks like a priest. He can't erase from his mind the clerical education he received and practiced for the greater part of his life. They do not go to church because he considers that he and Marie-Louise are "living in sin" and that consequently they cannot receive the Sacraments. Nonetheless, their home is a Christian one, where the children are taught charity, kindness, honesty — in short, love for thy neighbour and a sense of responsibility.

FIRST RETURN TO HANMER (NOVEMBER 1920)

Gertrude, Marie-Louise's daughter, hands me a tape on which she has recorded some recollections:

> Today is November the first [2004] and why this comes to mind, I will never know because my grandmother, mother's mother, died November 1, 1920. And she was just fifty-one years of age. And mother went to her funeral with my brother Joe who was two and a half years old at that time. So you can imagine the stir that it must have made in Hanmer when she was there, when she showed up for the funeral. There must have been a lot of talking going on. "Did you see who is there?" Anyhow, just reminiscences.[21]

How Marie-Louise must have been upset to learn of her mother's death! Did she ever have the opportunity to talk with her since she fled Hanmer and to explain to her the reasons for her departure? During the four preceding years, Marie-Louise in her quiet moments certainly imagined several times what she would tell her mother if she saw her again, the chat they would have and the confidences they would share. But now it is too late! Georgianne is gone. The only chance Marie-Louise has to silently tell her mother that she loves her and that she regrets having caused her sorrow is to go place a flower on her grave. And this time she won't wait until it is too late. Marie-Louise is firm about going to her mother's funeral. She does not know to what extent people in the village know her story. She is afraid to be asked questions by the village gossips. She certainly cannot reveal that she is living in common law with a man and that this man is, on top of that, the ex-curate of Hanmer. She would be immediately categorized as a loose woman and shunned by all scrupulous, conformist people. But the prospect of having to navigate in an explosive social environment does not stop her. She takes Joe with her and goes down to her sister Claire's to whom she has remained particularly attached and with whom she can openly share her grief. She possibly confides in her that she is pregnant once again.

Joseph does not accompany Marie-Louise to Hanmer. Someone has to stay home and look after the animals and the business. He probably also fears the reception he would get from Napoléon should he show up at the funeral. Marie-Louise decides to leave little Gertrude in her father's care.

BIRTH OF LORNE

Back from Hanmer, life returns to normal. On 16 March 1921, Marie-Louise gives birth to a second son. When I ask Gertrude where her young brother was born, she answers:

G: *Lorne; I think that he was born at home.*
C: *Ah! Did she have help?*
G: *She must have had a midwife, I suppose. In those
days I'm not sure how it worked. I don't really
know. It's something I always wondered about.
Who came to the house to help her?* [22]

A short research into the living habits of the day provides a plausible answer to this question. In the early 1900s, many women chose to give birth at home assisted by a midwife. In Marie-Louise's neighbourhood, it is a common practice and midwives are appreciated as much by the doctors as by the women giving birth, as revealed by the following testimony of a Billings Bridge inhabitant:

> *My grandmother ... was a midwife. She was as important as the Queen. All the doctors counted on her.
> If they knew that she was taking care of a case, they
> didn't bother to come.*[23]

It is thus quite possible that Marie-Louise receives help from a midwife while Joseph walks back and forth in the kitchen. As he had done for Joe and for Gertrude, Joseph baptizes the baby himself. He and Marie-Louise have chosen a very French name: Albert Laurent. However later on, since all his friends speak only English, Laurent will ask to be called Lorne.

1921–1926

The country's economy is gradually improving in the war's aftermath. Women's status is also improving. In 1917, suffragettes have earned the right for women to vote. Many women who worked outside the home during the war are reluctant to return to unpaid housework. The fairer sex feels the wind in its sails and fashion attests to it. Haircuts and hem lengths get shorter. In high society, cloche hats replace the large "My Fair Lady" hats ornate with ribbons and feathers. New conveniences, such as the famous Frigidaire refrigerator, come onto the market, making tasks easier for wives and mothers. *"Telephones are used more and more. Between 1915 and 1925, the number of telephones in Canada doubled. By 1925, more than 13% of Canadians are using Bell's invention."*[24]

In the Stanley Street home, Joseph and Marie-Louise might very well be contemplating some improvements to the house and might need additional money to do so because on 2 June 1925, Joseph sells, for an amount of $500, the second part of Lot 2, Concession II that he had bought in the township of Hanmer in 1913.

Days and months fly, punctuated with happy events that remain in the children's memory to this day. Gertrude recollects going to Carlsbad Springs with her father to get spring water.

> **G:** *We went there by buggy, you know. He would go there and take me with him. Sometimes he would bring Joe or Lorne.*
> **C:** *Each in turn.*
> **G:** *Yes, yes, that's right. It was a major excursion. It took the whole day you know.*
> **C:** *It's far.*
> **G:** *Yes.*
> **C:** *So you brought spring water back to the house?*
> **G:** *Oh yes.*[25]

These are carefree days, full of games: tag, hide and seek, hopscotch, marbles, skipping rope and spin the bottle. One day when Joseph is absent and Marie-Louise is busy, the boys go up to the attic. Their father keeps a trunk there and the boys are dying to know what it contains. They open it and find all the religious objects belonging to their father: a paten, a ciborium, a chalice, etc. But their amusement rises tenfold when they discover a rifle amongst these religious objects. One can wonder, of course, why a priest would own a gun. But Marie-Louise's niece explains to me:

> *In those days, it was normal for people to carry rifles, on the farm, to protect from bears, etc. Priest or no priest.*[26]

Sometimes, unexpected events occur and their reminiscence still makes one laugh. For example there is the day when Joseph bought a cow at the annual rodeo in Lansdowne Park. Gertrude and Lorne tell me:

> **L:** They had a rodeo, down at Lansdowne Park.
> And after the rodeo, they sold all the cows [that]
> the cowboys [used] to ride, something like that.
> Is that the way it went?
> **G:** Yeah.
> **L:** Something like that. So anyway, he bought one.
> And the cowboys brought it home. They herd
> the bugger and put it in the barn. He [Dad]
> goes out of the barn and closes the door, you
> know. And then the baker came along and [said],
> "It sounds the big deal you got with this cow.
> So let's go and have a look at it!" So they go out
> to the barn and mother comes along ...
> **G:** and she opened the door ...
> **L:** and the cow ran away![27]

It would seem that the cow, worried about its fate, considered it wise to make a bid for freedom and to seek refuge with the neighbours, the Billings. Gertrude and Lorne still laugh over the memory of their father galloping behind the cow to recapture it, just like in the finale of a Charlie Chaplin movie.

GERTRUDE'S FIRST COMMUNION

On 21 April 1926 Gertrude gets up with a mix of joy and apprehension in her heart. Today is her First Communion and her Confirmation. She is anxious to slip on the pretty dress that Marie-Louise has made for her. But at the same time, she is a bit apprehensive about having to go to church. She has never been there and doesn't know exactly what to expect.

> **G:** *My mother was sick that day and both my*
> *brothers had the mumps. So I went by myself. My*
> *father took me to the church in a horse and buggy.*
> *He left me*
> *at the door of the church and went away.*[28]
> **C:** *But were the other parents in the church?*
> **G:** *Oh, yes. The other children all had their parents*
> *present and they were all dressed in white with a*
> *veil and everything. And me, I was dressed with*
> *a blue dress, a beautiful dress that mother made*
> *for me, all embroidered with roses, I remember,*
> *very pretty. So that I felt … not with the gang,*
> *you know. And I remember that a woman, a nice*
> *woman with a dozen children, took care of me.*[29]

This woman is called Mrs. Brûlé. She brings Gertrude to her home for lunch and lends her a veil for the Confirmation that takes place the same day in the afternoon.

> **G:** *The First Communion was in the morning and*
> *the Confirmation was in the afternoon.*
> **C:** *On the same day?*
> **G:** *On the same day, because the Bishop made the*
> *rounds, that way. That's how it worked. And*
> *then my father came to get me afterwards.*[30]

This day stays carved in Gertrude's heart like a notch made with a knife in tree bark. She is 8 years old and it is the first time she realizes with unease that her family does not follow some of the social conventions of their neighbours.

> *You see, my mother had not been to church for many years. We did not belong to the parish. So these things were a bit different from everybody else.*[31]

It will not be the last time that her family situation causes her embarrassment.

FACING FACTS

During the weeks following Gertrude's First Communion, Marie-Louise's health continues to decline to the point where she must be hospitalized.

> **G:** *She had a hysterectomy ... In those days, it was a big operation ... And I remember that while she was in the hospital, [he] set up an altar in the hallway upstairs and he would say mass.*
> **C:** *In your house?*
> **G:** *Yes, yes, in our house. I remember that. It took up a lot of room because the hallway wasn't that wide. Anyway, I imagine that he was very worried.*
> **C:** *Did she stay in the hospital for a long time?*
> **G:** *A couple of weeks.*
> **C:** *So while she was in the hospital, he took care of you?*
> **G:** *Yes.*
> **C:** *And he got no help from the neighbours?*
> **G:** *I don't know. He was a pretty good cook, I suppose. With all the travelling that he did, he must have had to cook for himself in all those small places.*[32]

I can only imagine the impact on Joseph of having to take care of the children by himself. He suddenly realizes how much the household management depends on Marie-Louise: cooking, laundry, cleaning, and mending. On top of his work, he must now plan and prepare meals, answer the children's questions and oversee their activities. For the first time since they began living together, he is asking himself: what would happen if I lost Marie-Louise? He suddenly confronts the possibility of finding himself a widower at 68 years with sole responsibility for three children less than 10 years of age. This thought throws him into turmoil and deep inside he is overcome with secret fears. He fears that he might have chosen the wrong path in his life. He fears that he got himself and Marie-Louise into an adventure that makes no sense. He fears to face the doubts eating away at his heart.

The only recourse he knows for confronting fear is prayer. He climbs to the attic, opens his trunk, takes out and holds the religious objects he had put away at a euphoric moment in his life. His heart is pounding. These familiar objects speak to him of calm, silence and inner peace. He sees himself back then saying mass in the little chapel of Wolseley, out in Saskatchewan. He hears the altar boy softly answering: *"Kyrie eleison." "God, have pity."* He thinks, *"I am a priest. There! There is the truth. I am a priest and I will always be one."* This certitude suddenly appears like a beacon amongst the doubts casting a shadow over his thoughts and brings him inner peace. Calmed, he goes downstairs and erects an altar in the hallway. He must have faith in the future. During the mass that he celebrates under the astounded looks of his children, what does he promise to God in exchange for Marie-Louise's recovery?

SYNCHRONICITY

Marie-Louise comes home and resumes managing the household. The storm has abated. Joseph can now truly value his wife's hard work and must surely tell her so more often, which makes her happy. Months pass and numerous events make the headlines in Ottawa. They keep conversations going in the household and provide the opportunity to go on nice outings. For instance, in August 1926, Ottawa celebrates its centennial. Many festivities take place and people hurry to see the military parade and the floats. In 1927, the city cinemas present *The Jazz Singer*, the very first talking film. It's quite possible that the family went to see it. Marie-Louise adores movies!

Then Joseph begins to receive frequent visits from a neighbour, Mr. Christie. This married man has many children. He is also a Minister in a Church that allows priests to marry. He might be Protestant, Presbyterian, or Anglican, I don't know. Gertrude says to me that each time he came over to the house, Joseph and he had long conversations. What do they discuss so intensely? They possibly debate whether priests should marry. Joseph would love to be able to rationalize his dilemma of being a Catholic priest and living in a common-law relationship with a woman he can't marry for threat of excommunication. He would prefer not to be forced to choose between saving his soul and staying with his loved ones for whom he feels responsible. He is most certainly interested in the beliefs and rituals of his neighbour's religion. So there are religions where you can consecrate yourself to God while being married? Marie-Louise leaves both men to their discussions but undoubtedly feels a little insecure when she sees Joseph so captivated by the topic.

And, as if by coincidence, news concerning the Catholic Church soon makes the newspapers' headlines. On 28 March 1928 Monsignor Guillaume Forbes is named Archbishop of Ottawa. Joseph surely talks about this with Marie-Louise over the supper table. She listens to him with interest as she always does when he reports the latest news. She is not surprised that Joseph takes special notice of this news, but she is far from suspecting that this Archbishop's arrival in the Capital will provoke an upheaval in her life.

Joseph has a very good reason to be particularly interested in the news. Monsignor Forbes was ordained on 17 March 1888, by Monsignor Fabre. Joseph had also been ordained by Monsignor Fabre, only three weeks earlier, on 26 February 1888. Guillaume Forbes and Joseph were therefore colleagues in the Great Seminary. Does Joseph entertain the idea of renewing his links with him? Given the long conversations he has had recently with his neighbour, we can assume that he has not yet rid himself of the ambiguity that prevails in his heart. Meeting Monsignor Forbes would give him the opportunity to discreetly discuss his situation with a Church representative. He could ask for his opinion and informally explore with him possible solutions to his dilemma.

THE BIG DECISION (1928)

What follows is only speculation on my part, as Marie-Louise brought Joseph's story to her grave. We can surmise that he meets with Monsignor Forbes and that the latter adopts a very clear stance. He reminds him of the proverb from the Bible: *He who has a crooked heart finds no happiness.*[33] He unequivocally demonstrates to him that his duty is to save his soul by giving himself to God only. Finally, he assures this "lost son" that the Church is ready to open its doors to him on certain conditions, the first being that he leaves forever this woman that he has not married and their illegitimate children.

This unambiguous position seems logical to Joseph if he is to save his soul. He understands it because he received the same education that his colleague received and his fundamental beliefs have not changed over the years. He is tempted to follow this course. Moreover, he thinks that the quiet life of a man of the cloth will suit him better at age 70 than the daily struggle of making a living for a woman and three young children. But he feels pangs of guilt at the idea of abandoning Marie-Louise and leaving her the responsibility to raise their children alone. He wants to ensure that if he returns to the priesthood, he will have put in place the means to protect them one way or another. It is therefore highly probable that he negotiates with the Church an arrangement to that effect.

Joseph spends the days following this encounter on the "Mount of Olives." He knows now what he wants to do. But he wonders if he will ever find the courage to go through with it. Finally, he comes clean with Marie-Louise, describes to her his internal dilemma and narrates to her his visit with Monsignor Forbes. Could she understand and forgive him if he should return to the priesthood?

Marie-Louise's happiness crumbles like a house of cards in a gust of wind.

CHAPTER FIVE

1928 TO *1935*

"Widow" with Three Children

> Since that's the way it is, we'll get
> through it, and we will do what we
> need to do. That is my life; that is life!
>
> ♂ MARIE-LOUISE

HEARTBREAK

He is gone. Marie-Louise can hardly believe it. In the days leading up to his departure she no doubt must have riddled him with questions. How will she manage the household on a daily basis without him? She, who barely knows how to read and write, how will she earn a living? He gave her a few instructions on managing the household budget. He revealed to her that he was keeping hidden in the basement, in the space between the ceiling joists and the wall, a metal box containing Canada Savings Bonds for the children's education. He promised to make all the necessary arrangements for her to become owner of the house and the lots.

In the following days, the children ask where their father is.

> We didn't know where he was or why he was gone.
> Mother, she knew, but she never talked about it. And
> the minute that we asked questions she started to cry,
> so naturally we stopped asking.[1]

She cannot explain where their father is gone. He made her promise to never talk about him to anyone, not even to their children. So she promised, not anticipating all the consequences that this promise would have on her life in the future. She has buried deep in her heart forever the secret of their love story. The children do not know that their father was a priest before they were born. They cannot grasp the reason for this sudden absence. Worried, they gradually realize that something very serious has occurred and that there is no use insisting on explanations. None will be obtained from their mother.

Now an adult, Gertrude understands all of the emotions underlying her mother's silence:

> … how lonely she must have been after my father
> left us! She never, never spoke of it, of Dad at all,

and I am sure she must have thought about him a lot.[2]

Marie-Louise has lost the love of her life. She has lost face in front of the very society that she had defied. Her self-esteem has taken a major hit. She finds herself alone to raise three young children. Many women would have sunk into a deep depression if such a misfortune had happened to them. Not Marie-Louise. Thanks to the strength of her character, she is soon back at the helm. Her niece tells me, *"She was very determined. She would say, 'Since that's the way it is, we'll get through it, and we will do what we need to do. That is my life; that is life!'"*[3]

UNEXPECTED VISITS

While sipping tea with Gertrude, I continue to ask her about the period immediately following her father's departure. Did she ever see him again?

> G: *Well, he came to see us a couple of times during the first year after he left.*
> C: *Oh, so he came back to the house?*
> G: *Yes.*

She adds in the written document that she hands to me, "We were so glad to see him!" But their father only stays for a few hours, and then leaves.

> C: *He came wearing his Roman collar?*
> G: *Yes. And so I said "Why are you wearing that?" you know. And he laughed and turned it around backwards as a joke, you understand. So, in fact …*[4]

If Joseph has promised the Church that he will cease all contact with his family, it is surprising that he returns for short visits. But I surmise that he received special permission from the Church so as to make the financial arrangements necessary to protect his family. During these short visits, Marie-Louise experiences the bittersweet hope that any woman in love and jilted by her lover feels when she sees him again after the separation. To her great joy, he is there in front of her. She would like to throw her arms around his neck and hold him tightly to her. But he smiles at her while keeping his distance, like a visiting priest. He asks about her and the children. He tells her that he has started the process to put the house and lots in her name and that there will be papers for her to sign. He leaves her an address where she can return the signed documents. And he departs again leaving her sadly disappointed. The sound of the door closing reverberates in the emptiness around her. Her heart is bleeding. Just as she was beginning to feel a little bit stronger, she now feels vulnerable once more.

For the children, too, these visits are a source of interrogation and emotional turmoil.

> C: *When he came to visit one day, you must have*
> *asked him, "Where are you coming from?"*
> *How did you explain this to yourselves?*
> G: *We imagined all kinds of things but we didn't*
> *know. And we couldn't talk about it with mother.*
> *So there was emptiness there, all the time! It wasn't*
> *funny you know, when you think about it! [Some]*
> *children in the neighbourhood where saying,*
> "Your father is a priest!"
> C: *How did they know?*
> G: *Oh well, I imagine that a lot of people knew about*
> *it. Because for one thing, when he came to visit us,*
> *he would walk from the Billings Station to the house*

*wearing his Roman collar. In those days, everyone
knew one another, so I am sure that everybody knew
about it. I don't know what they thought. They
didn't talk about it. Oh no, no one talked about it.*
C: *But the children, they talked about it.*
G:. *Oh, that was when we were in primary school,
you know, and he hadn't been gone long.*
C: *So your neighbours were discreet.*
G: *For sure, yes. They were good neighbours. Good
Protestants.*[5]

LIVING DAY TO DAY

Daily life continues without interval of rest for Marie-Louise, like
a wind that one would like to see drop but that keeps on blow-
ing. Joseph's absence makes the task harder. On top of her usual
household chores, Marie-Louise is now responsible for the work
that Joseph used to do.

> After my father left, I think about all the work that
> my mother had to do on her own. In those days,
> you had to put the storm windows on for the win-
> ter, take them off again in the spring. And she had
> a garden. There was a lot of work there. And for
> the washing, you had to heat your water in a dou-
> ble boiler. And in the wintertime, we would close
> the summer kitchen and we would live in the living
> room, dining room area, which wasn't very large but
> of course there were four of us and we had a four-
> bedroom house at that time. Mother had a Singer
> sewing machine. I believe that was the only mark
> there was in those days. And it had a foot pedal.
> How she managed to make all the things she did

with this machine is a wonder to me. She made all our clothes. She was a wonderful seamstress and a good provider, a good cook.[6]

Joe is now old enough to help out with certain chores, like installing the storm windows. But it is not enough. Marie-Louise comes to realize that she can't do it all and that it is necessary to lighten the load.

> C: *Did she also take care of the animals you had?*
> G: *Well, when my father left, we got rid of them all.*
> C: *But you kept the dog.*
> G: *Certainly, yes! We kept the dog, and we kept some chickens for a little while, you know, not a long time.*[7]

The mood in the house has changed. Folk songs have been replaced with long silences full of ghostly dialogue.

> *And ... you know, since she never talked about what was going on, there weren't many conversations in our house. When everything is kept hidden like that, you end up not talking very much. In fact, I think it was boring, really.*[8]

Marie-Louise realizes how difficult it is to raise children on her own. Her days are so full that she can't keep track of their activities during the day, especially those of the boys who are not lacking for imagination in their games. A Rideau Park inhabitant, Allan Robertson, remembers a game Joe invented one winter:

> Joe Ray made a bobsled and after an ice storm, when the roads were slick, Joe and his brother, Lorne, and myself would whiz down Pleasant Park Road. We

crossed the tracks and flew down the steep hill and
prayed that there was no vehicles [sic] proceeding
in either direction on the River Road.[9]

If Marie-Louise had known about these blind bobsled rides, she
would have worried herself sick! In the spring, the boys also try
to hide from her their swims in a local quarry, but in vain! When
they return, she knows it right away, to their great surprise. But she
doesn't scold them. Lorne shares his memories with me:

> She was very liberal with us. In everything. In early
> spring, we used to go swimming in the shale pit on
> Smith Road. It was a hole dug to make the shale to
> make bricks. Jack mentioned that the other day. We
> used to worry about our hair being dry. We wondered
> if she would see our hair being wet, you know. And
> he said, Oh! That was you who were worried [about
> her noticing your wet hair] because the only thing she
> had to do is look at your neck and it was clean![10]

He chuckles just thinking about Marie-Louise's sagacity.

FREE TO EXPLORE LIFE

In the year immediately following Joseph's departure, Marie-Louise does not seem worried about finances. Yet she no longer has the
income from the sales of eggs and milk. I ask Gertrude how she
managed daily expenses.

> *I don't know. I think she had money in the bank. In
> those days — don't ask me how I remember this — she
> had $5,000. And in that era, $5,000 was a lot of
> money. So we lived quite well.*[11]

The federal Department of Labour had stated that a family needed between $1,200 and $1,500 per year to maintain a minimal standard of living.[12] With $5,000 Marie-Louise can live more comfortably than most of the population. She is sheltered from financial worries for a few years if she manages her money properly. Gertrude would be hard put to explain where this money came from, but she clearly remembers the amount. Perhaps Joseph left Marie-Louise some savings stemming in part from the sale of the lots he bought in Hanmer and Capreol townships and from his egg business. Joseph lived close to the bone when he was a missionary out West and he understood the importance of savings. He probably kept close ties on the family purse strings.

> *I think he believed that his money wouldn't last long and so we should be careful. And, in those days, there were no pensions. So you had to take care of yourself. But she had been raised on a farm. She knew nothing. So she … she splurged on spending. She dressed well. She had very good taste. And we [the children] didn't suffer either, naturally.*[13]

In certain respects, Marie-Louise maybe feels that she is free from Joseph's tight budgeting. She has never known life as a bachelor nor the freedom of deciding for herself the purchasing priorities. She discovers the pleasure of offering herself and offering to the children a bit more than just the bare essentials. She regularly receives the Eaton's catalogue. At that time, department stores such as Eaton's in English Canada and Dupuis & Frères in French Canada made the greater parts of their sales by catalogue. These catalogues displayed everything in the store with photos, sizes, measurements and prices. Men's and women's fashions, sporting goods, toys, tools, furniture and appliances would make everybody dream, the men as much as the women and children. Every year, people impatiently waited the arrival of the new catalogue. And when it arrived, everyone was trying to be the first to leaf through it.

In Marie-Louise's case, she discovers in the catalogue a whole range of activities that she has never tried before. Attracted by all novelties, she does not content herself with dreaming. She takes action.

> **G:** *When we lived on Pleasant Park, you know, she tried all kinds of new things and it was all through the Eaton's catalogue. It was the only place where one could buy. So after my father was gone, well, she bought an organ with pedals.*
>
> **C:** *Yes, yes.*
>
> **G:** *She bought that. And that satisfied her for a while. Then she switched it for a piano. Then she bought a harp [a small table-sized one]. And, of course they sent lessons with those. So she was trying to learn music by herself. She would try all kinds of things like that. And then painting, she always painted and some of it was painting on silk. Anyway, she always had something to interest her.*[14]

The catalogue allows her to explore more than just her penchant for artistic activities. She draws from it ideas for clothing and for the children's Christmas presents.

> **G:** *I remember that I received a doll, an Eaton's Beauty. I think that she had brown hair. Naturally, I thought she was gorgeous. And mother would sew all kinds of clothes for her. Really beautiful outfits!*
>
> **C:** *Did the doll have long or short hair?*
>
> **G:** *Long. You could comb it out. ... It was very special, I'm telling you!*[15]

Marie-Louise, Joseph, and Gertrude and her Eaton Beauty doll, circa 1930

Gertrude smiles tenderly as she reminisces how important this toy was to her little girl's heart. It is probably also in Eaton's catalogue that Marie-Louise gleans ideas to decorate Gertrude's bedroom.

> **G:** *She was always decorating the rooms. So my room was all pink. Even the floor! It was a linoleum floor. She had painted it pink and had added a border of all kinds of tiny flowers. When I think about it, it was a little too much pink!*
>
> [We laugh together.]
>
> **C:** *So now, as an adult, you wouldn't like it, but as a child you did?*
>
> **G:** *Oh yes, I thought it was beautiful!*
>
> **C:** *And she made pink curtains?*
>
> **G:** *Pink curtains with blue flowers in them!*
>
> **C:** *And the bedspread?*
>
> **G:** *Right. Everything! It all matched!*[16]

Of course, the catalogue continues to make the children dream all year long:

G: *We loved it! We selected everything we wanted even though we knew we weren't going to get them.* [We laugh together.] *It's the same today when children look at toy store flyers.*

C: *Oh yes! So you spent a lot of time looking in this catalogue?*

G: *Oh yes, yes.*

C: *And she didn't mind? She let you play with the catalogue?*

G: *Yes, yes. Because she got a new one every year, you know. And afterwards it made its way to the outhouse where we used it as toilet paper.*

C: *I see. Nothing got wasted!* [17]

[We laugh together once again.]

Marie-Louise's relaxed attitude around money in the year following Joseph's departure reflects well the general mentality of the population, who during the 1920s — until 1929 to be precise — profit from Canada's economic prosperity. Unemployment rate decreases and salaries increase. People don't worry about spending.

NAPOLÉON'S VISIT

After Joseph's departure, Marie-Louise reconnects with her family in Hanmer. Her adoptive father, Napoléon, comes for a visit. No doubt that Marie-Louise is extremely touched by this visit since she reads into it the proud Napoléon's discreet way of saying to her that bygones should be bygones, that he still loves her and that he is there for her if she needs help. She feels as if she has been welcomed back within the family fold.

THE CRASH, 24 OCTOBER 1929

In October 1929, newspapers are predicting an economic downturn. Marie-Louise is not sufficiently literate to read the papers on a regular basis. And had she read them, what would these troubles in the macroeconomics of the country have meant for her? Thus, when she hears on Thursday, 24 October about the New York stock market crash, Marie-Louise probably doesn't grasp right away the importance of this news. Sure, around her people are talking about fortunes vanishing overnight and about some rich financial magnates committing suicide. But all that seems far away.

From his secret hideaway, Joseph, who surely understands the importance of the situation, writes often to Marie-Louise, probably to brief her on his financial arrangements, to explain to her the dangers of the economic situation in the country, and to urge her to avoid superfluous expenses. She answers him. Gertrude tells me that she never saw the content of the letters written by her mother but that the address on the envelope caught her attention.

> *When she was giving me a letter to mail, it was always to "J.A. Roy." She wrote "R-O." And I would tell her, "Look you put an o here; it should be an a." And she would reply, "Oh, never mind. Just go mail it! Mail it!" you know. So that is the only glimpse of the secret that she uncovered, without realizing it. And we didn't make anything of it.*[18]

In returning to the priesthood, Joseph took back his real family name, Roy, thereby psychologically distancing himself even more from Marie-Louise and the children who are still called "Ray." But Marie-Louise does her best to keep them in touch with him. She keeps sending him news of the children and, for a short period of time, he stays in contact with them. Gertrude recollects:

G: *He wrote me a few letters after he left.*

C: *Oh, really! Do you still have them?*

G: *No, we moved around so often that we didn't keep very much.*

C: *What did he say in those letters?*

G: *Oh well …* [She raises her hands in the air in a gesture of powerlessness]

C: *Did he give any explanations?*

G: *No. But if I was getting good grades in school or if I was first in my class, he would send me a paper 25-cent note. We called those "shin plasters." And I thought that I was really wealthy!* [19]

She laughs remembering this childhood delight.

Joseph doesn't forget to mark his daughter's birthday. And with good reason! It is the same day as his own birthday. During one of our interviews, Gertrude shows me what she received from her father in the mail for her birthday on 30 October 1929.

G: *I only have one thing with his writing on it. It is the only souvenir of him that I have.*

C: *What is it? A letter?*

G: *Let me show you.*

She gets up and goes into her room to fetch something. She returns with a framed picture of Saint Theresa the Little Flower, on the back of which it is hand-written, "I pray for you." And the date inscribed on the picture is "1929."

G: *This was after he had gone.*

C: *Right because he left in 1928. So there was still a little bit of contact in 1929.* [20]

FAMILY TIES

In the summer of 1930, Marie-Louise decides to visit her sister Claire in Blezard Valley near Sudbury, and to bring her children. She makes an arrangement with her neighbour, Mr. Bennett, to drive them there. To finance the trip, she rents her house to a couple named Baker, who are looking for a place to stay with their four children while waiting to buy a new home. Gertrude remembers the trip to Blezard Valley:

> **G:** *Mr. Bennett drove us to Sudbury. He had a* Model T Ford *with a* rumble seat. *Do you know what that is?*
> **C:** *It's like a seat behind in the trunk?*
> **G:** *Yes, exactly. Just imagine! There were six of us: Joe, Lorne, me, mother, Mr. Bennett and his older son, Chad. I'm telling you we were so crowded! And it took us two days. It was quite a trip. Mother almost got sick afterwards. Mr. Bennett took us to my aunt Claire's in Blezard Valley and then he returned. We stayed for a month at the Bergeron's. It was the first time that we visited true relatives.*[21]

Napoléon receives the family for dinner in Hanmer and serves a surprise dish, keeping the recipe secret until the end of the meal. When all are pleasantly full and jealous cooks are begging him to reveal his recipe, he triumphantly announces that they just ate a stew of bear meat.

Marie-Louise and the children are delighted to find themselves with relatives. They have missed this life style. The children are surprised by the number of cousins they have. Joe and Gertrude communicate with all these people in French, but Lorne, whom everyone calls Laurent, is uncomfortable expressing himself in French and, although he understands very well what is said, he answers in English.

After spending all of August at Aunt Claire's, Marie-Louise and the children come back to Ottawa by train. This first visit with their relatives opened a new era in the relationship between Marie-Louise and her family. From this moment on, aunts, uncles, nieces and nephews start coming in turn to Ottawa for weeks at a time and Marie-Louise often goes back to visit them.

A surprise awaits their arrival in Ottawa. The Bakers still have not found a new house and ask if they can stay a few more weeks. Marie-Louise doesn't have the heart to evict them. Generous neighbours, the Labrèches, offer to put her up with her children. She accepts and assures them it is only for a short period of time. But the Depression has stalled the real estate market and it becomes obvious that the Bakers will not soon find a home. Marie-Louise does not want to abuse the Labrèches' hospitality. She returns to her home and reorganizes the allocation of the rooms to accommodate both families. She installs Mr. and Mrs. Baker in the first small bedroom, Lorne and Joe in the second, and the two Baker boys in the third. Then she puts Gertrude and the two Baker girls in the large room over the summer kitchen. As for herself, she sleeps on a couch in the living room. Everybody is cramped for room but their situation seems quite enviable to others literally put out on the street by the Great Depression.

Homeowner

While Marie-Louise has been up north visiting her relatives, Joseph has taken the necessary steps to transfer to her the title deed for the house and the lots on Stanley Street. The notarized documents indicate that on 16 August 1930, Joseph *Roy* sells his lots to Marie-Louise *Ray* for $1,500. Marie-Louise signs "Marie-Louise *Ray*, widow." The notary doesn't seem to notice the fact that the property was first bought by a Mr. *Ray* and is now sold by a Mr. *Roy*. Perhaps he takes for granted that the name change is merely a typo? Whatever the case, the documents are certified.

IMPACT OF JOSEPH'S DEPARTURE

Gertrude tries to help me understand the physical and emotional consequences of Joseph's departure on her and her brothers.

> G: *We missed him, you know. … It's a strange*
> *situation when you think about it.* [short silence]
> *It was sad. Yes, you know when other children*
> *spoke of their father or mother. And us, we couldn't*
> *talk about our father. Children would ask us. I told*
> *a lot of fibs … I would say, "He had a heart attack"*
> *or … A lot of things happened to him! … I don't*
> *know what people thought about us really. Anyway!*
> *There was always a hole there, all the time!*
> C: *This hole was emotional, not just physical.*
> G: *Yes, yes. In fact, I think it affected me. And the*
> *boys. Joe more than Lorne, I think, I'm not sure*
> *why. Maybe because he was the eldest and he*
> *remembered our father more. … There was just a*
> *big void there, all the time. And I don't know how*
> *one can describe this. There was no one with whom*
> *I could talk about it, you know. If relatives had*
> *been nearby* [with whom] *to talk to. But there was*
> *no one!*[22]

I asked her what her reaction was when she understood that her father would never return.

> *Really, when you think about it. I hated him for a long*
> *time, but afterwards … My oldest brother, Joe, he is*

dead now, but he never, ever forgave him. He always
hated him. He called him, "That son of a … " [23]

Diane, Joe's daughter, confirms this in telling me about her father's
relationship with his father:

> **D:** He hated his father because, when it happened,
> he was the oldest and he felt completely abandoned
> and he saw how my grandmother's heart was
> broken. And his heart was broken too! He was old
> enough. And he just resented him. He hated him
> and could never say a nice word about him.
> **C:** What else did he tell you about your grandfather?
> **D:** I can't repeat it! No I mean, he used to use
> actually not nice words whenever I asked anything
> about him. [24]

As for Lorne, he was still too young in 1928 to fully realize the
impact of Joseph's departure. However, later, when Joe and Gertrude had left home, he stayed alone with his mother and became
an invaluable support for her during the rough times they went
through together.

Gertrude still doesn't know the reasons why her father returned
to the priesthood. She puts forward some plausible explanations,
but she knows full well that it is only speculation on her part.

> *Well, after having had children at his age it must have*
> *been difficult, very complicated. And I imagine that*
> *he felt stuck, with three young kids. And then, I don't*
> *know what happened, whether the Church contacted*
> *him or he contacted them. Anyway, they might have*
> *paid him to return, I don't know.* [25]

In the next interview, as we come back to the subject, she adds:

> G: *Well, he went back and he was a teaching.*
> C: *Oh really. What was he teaching?*
> G: *Well, very Catholic stuff I suppose. I don't really know, I just heard that he was supposed to be teaching. I don't know where I heard that.*
> C: *It's Marie-Louise that is whispering the answers to you.*
> [She laughs and adds in a determined tone of voice.]
> G: *Well, she should have spoken a long time ago!*[26]

Later on, the extended family will try to understand the motiva-tion behind his departure, but will only be able to suggest some hypotheses:

> GB: *My mother* [her mother was Marie-Louise's sister], *her name was Claire, always said, "If his superiors had left him alone, he would never have left Marie-Louise ... [and] the children would have had a father."*
> C: *So you think his superiors put pressure on him?*
> GB: *My mother always said so, and I heard it very, very often.*[27]

Only Marie-Louise knows the real reasons why Joseph returned to the priesthood, and she kept the secret forever.

RELIGION AFTER JOSEPH'S DEPARTURE

In talking with Gertrude about the impact of her father's depar-ture, of course the topic of religion came up.

C: *My Lord, she must have sat, at night, and dammed*
   this God that took her husband from her?
G: *Never, never did she speak against religion.*
   Never.[28]

If Marie-Louise feels bitterness about the Church and the Catholic religion, she doesn't let it show. In spite of her sorrow, she seems to accept the situation, as one accepts an extraordinary event beyond belief, an event that cannot be fully understood. Brought up in the Catholic faith, she learned to submit to "God's will." Moreover, she certainly does not want her personal views to influence her children's religious life. Hence her decision to return to her religious practice after Joseph left.

G: *When Dad was living with us, we did not go*
   to mass.
C: *Never?*
G: *Never. … Well, he did not go to mass, so mother*
   didn't go either. So we became Catholic again
   after his departure.[29]

We laugh together because she says this last sentence very simply, as if declaring that she has decided to put on again a previously discarded shirt. I have no doubt that Gertrude inherited from her mother her sense of humour and the graceful attitude with which she accepts life's detours.

THE FRENCH–ENGLISH QUESTION

Joseph's departure leads to another unexpected consequence: the spoken language at home slips gradually from French to English, as if the household had lost its anchor with the French language. I ask Gertrude:

C: *On Stanley Avenue, when your father was there,*
did you speak French or English in the house?
G: *We spoke French. But after he left we spoke*
English.
C: *When he was there, your neighbours were*
anglophones?
G: *They were all anglophones.*
C: *So, in the house you spoke French and when*
you went out you spoke English?
G: Yes.
C: *And then when he left?*
G: *It was all English. Mother was trying to speak*
French to us, but we would answer in English.
C: *Because you were going to English schools?*
G: *Yes, exactly. … And then herself, you know,*
she spoke better English than French.[30]

Obviously, all of Marie-Louise's friends are anglophones. Only with Mr. Brûlé, the butcher, can she speak French. So gradually her English improves and her French starts to fade.

LIFE DURING THE GREAT DEPRESSION

In the years following the Crash, the Depression deepens throughout Canada. The Government must create programs to help out the poor. In Ottawa, the Depression is felt unevenly across the population. The Public Service offers relatively stable work, although many public servants still lose their jobs. In April 1932, the Government imposes a 10% salary cut on federal public servants.[31] Thankfully, since the cost of living is also falling, most of them can still support their families. As for workers in private industry and trade, they face massive layoffs.

In 1930, Marie-Louise does not feel the Depression's disastrous after-effects as much as most citizens across the country. Of course, the Bakers can't move and everyone feels crowded in the Stanley Avenue home. But they make do. Since the house is in a rural setting, the household can mostly feed itself with produce from the garden and the orchard, protecting them from the scarcity others encounter in the city.

With a household of ten people, Marie-Louise realizes that if she wants to accomplish everything she needs to do, she will have to find a means of transportation for weekly errands and for outings with friends and family. As usual, she does not hesitate to take action.

> *Mother bought a car, a Pontiac '29. One of our neighbours, Mr. Crouch, taught her to drive. In those days, you didn't need to pass a driver's test or anything. So she was driving. She was the only woman in the neighbourhood who was driving an automobile.*[32]

One wonders how Marie-Louise had enough money to buy a car. Maybe she found a bargain. Indeed, when the Depression arrived many businessmen were ruined overnight. Some of them sold their cars for a ridiculously low amount just to get some cash. Perhaps someone told Marie-Louise that she could buy a practically new automobile for next to nothing and she jumped on the deal. The rent paid by the Bakers probably also helped finance the purchase.

BANK STREET (1930–1932) AND SUNNYSIDE STREET (1932–1933)

Although, Marie-Louise has owned the house and lots since the fall of 1930, she has no regular income for day-to-day expenses. The financial cushion Joseph left her is dwindling away.

She was spending money and no money was coming in, so you know …[33]

The Depression continues to worsen and Marie-Louise must confront its menacing countenance more and more. First, she hears perturbing news reports, including one about the May 1931 suicide of Ottawa's Chief of Police, Charles Hopewell, overwhelmed by financial problems.[34] Then she starts witnessing the Depression's impact in the streets in Ottawa. People walk everywhere, since they have no money to take public transportation or, if they own a car, to fill the gas tank. In doing her errands, Marie-Louise sees the beneficiaries of the "dole," or Government aid, queuing up at grocery stores to exchange their coupons for a piece of meat or a bag of sugar. She notices in passing the great number of youth swelling the ranks at soup kitchen doors and thinks about Joe who will, before too long, be looking for work also. She resorts to using credit, too. She buys her groceries at J.L. Brûlé's in Billings Bridge and can't always pay the full amount at the cash register. The owner allows her to wait until the end of the month to settle her account.

Finally, Marie-Louise can't make ends meet with the little cash she has left. She must find a source of income. Since the Bakers are still sharing the Stanley Avenue house, she decides to rent them the whole house and to go live elsewhere on the proceeds from their rent. She and the children move to the second floor apartment of a house located behind a diner on Bank Street, between Cameron and Riverdale in Ottawa South. On the ground floor live a Jewish man, his wife and child. This man rents and operates the diner attached to the house. Lorne and Gertrude tell me:

> **L:** The Jewish lad and his wife had a child. They
> were living downstairs, we were living upstairs.
> And, all of a sudden, one morning, he is gone
> with the family! The guy walked away. He left

everything there. … And then, when the Jewish
lad moved out, we took the whole house.

G: … and the store.[35]

Marie-Louise takes over the lunch counter. She rents one room in
the house to a labourer who owns a horse and Gertrude has to rise
early every morning to prepare this man's breakfast. Marie-Louise
does not make her fortune with the store.

G: *It was only a* corner store.

C: *Like a confectionary?*

G: *Not exactly a confectionary because she didn't sell
food products, really. It was mostly chocolate bars
and sodas. … There were a couple of tables. Val
[Lorne's wife] remembers going there with her
brother; they bought a chocolate bar, sat at the table
and split the bar in two, you know. So,* big treat! [36]
[She laughs.]

Marie-Louise operates the small lunch counter for a year or two.
But she has no business experience and the Depression worsens
relentlessly. Her business slowly dries up. Soon, she does not have
enough income to pay the rent for the house and the store. Since
the Bakers still occupy the house on Stanley Avenue, she must find
another place to live. While the children finish their school year
at Saint Margaret Mary's, Marie-Louise sets out to find other ac-
commodation.

In 1932, she and the children move to the second floor of a house
at 402 Sunnyside. As the homeowner, Mr. Patterson, pays his taxes
for the public school system, come September Marie-Louise must
enroll the children in the Hopewell Public School. One day, upon
returning from school, Gertrude finds her mother in tears. Are financial worries the cause of Marie-Louise's sorrow? Gertrude will

never know because, as usual, her mother remains silent about the reasons for her actions and feelings. Thankfully, the sojourn on Sunnyside is a short one. In the spring of 1933, Marie-Louise and the children move back to their home on Stanley Avenue. The Bakers still live there, and they continue to do so until the fall, when Mr. Baker buys a fairly large property on River Road, at Uplands, to start raising chickens.

402 Sunnyside Street

STANLEY AVENUE (1933–1935)

The country's economic situation just keeps on getting worse. One Canadian in five depends on Government aid programs. Unemployed men illicitly travel the railroad from one end of the country to the other, in the hopes of finding work. They stop in one city or another, knock at doors to offer their services in exchange for a meal, and leave by train for other towns. Near Marie-Louise's house in Billings Bridge, many jobless men who come in by train from the West form a rustic campground. An Ottawa citizen tells me:

> There were hundreds of them out there at Billings Bridge, you know, living in tents and everything else. Well, make shift. I don't think they all had tents.[37]

Soon, they come to knock at Marie-Louise's door. Gertrude recollects:

> G: *I remember that during the Depression, people often came by … They were looking for work. If there was no work, then [they would ask], "Can you give me something to eat?"*
>
> C: *They knocked at your door?*
>
> G: *Yes, yes. She always gave them something to eat. … We didn't live far from the tracks. So they just got off there, I suppose. And they walked around, looking for work …*
>
> C: *And your mother fed them with what?*
>
> G: *Well, with sandwiches.*[38]

In the hopes of reducing the vagrancy of jobless people in Ottawa, the government establishes a work camp in Rockliffe to build a road. This work provides a few very low-paying jobs but does nothing to lessen the devastating impact of the Depression. In 1934, 22,000 people depend on Government aid in the nation's capital.[39] Women abandoned by their husbands and left to raise children on their own easily slide under the threshold of poverty.

Marie-Louise receives no Government assistance at all because she can't prove that she is a widow. Since she promised to never reveal her past life, she fears the questions that may await her, were she to ask for aid.

And of course, in those days, what she has done was such
a mortal sin that she couldn't speak about it to anyone,
you know. So she couldn't go ask for assistance.[40]

She makes do as best she can. With the Canada Savings Bonds that
Joseph left, she enrolls Gertrude at Rideau Street Convent and Joe
at the Ottawa Technical School. However, since she no longer receives an income from renting the house, her dire financial straits
are becoming increasingly worse. It is therefore possible that she
may have decided to ask Joseph for financial help, because in the
next two years she makes numerous trips to Montreal.

> *We went to Montreal several times. She went to meet*
> *[someone] — we didn't know whom — we thought that*
> *she met with father but she didn't say, we didn't know*
> *what she was doing. Anyway, we parked on Sherbrooke*
> *Street, and she left us in the car. It was a big building,*
> *and I wonder if it wasn't the Seminary. She would en-*
> *ter, and we waited in the car for her. We had no idea*
> *what was going on. I don't know if she was going to*
> *see him, or if it was to decide how to solve our finan-*
> *cial problems. I don't know. ... And she never stayed*
> *very long. When she returned, she was very sad. And,*
> *anyway, we would do all that in one day.*[41]

These trips to Montreal were the source of many discussions during my interviews with Gertrude and her brother Lorne. Lorne
recalls that when Marie-Louise was leaving the building she had
in her hands an envelope full of money. Was this money coming from Joseph or from the Church? Gertrude and Lorne suspect that, as part of the agreement negotiated by Joseph with the
Church for his return to the priesthood, he obtained that the
Church would financially compensate Marie-Louise in return

for her silence on her life with him. Gertrude tells me, "It was 'hush money'."[42]

Given how important it was to the Church to keep Joseph's "straying" a secret, in order to hush up the scandal, this interpretation of events makes sense. But we have no way of verifying its accuracy.

Gertrude notices how sad her mother is when she leaves the Seminary. With good reason! During her first trip to Montreal, she is probably going there secretly hoping to have the pleasure of seeing Joseph again and of conversing a little with him. But since the Church made Joseph promise to never see her again, I suspect that Joseph was obliged to leave the envelope with some receptionist who handed it over to Marie-Louise in a very impersonal manner, maybe even with a half suspicious, half disdainful look. How humiliating for such a proud woman to be perceived as a beggar. So for Marie-Louise, these trips to Montreal are synonyms for disappointment and humiliation. For the children, these trips are rather fun. It is an adventure out of their daily life. They stop for lunch at a restaurant, a real treat for them. Furthermore, for Joe, who is now 16 and has started to drive, it is a golden opportunity to practice a bit.

According to Gertrude, Marie-Louise would have gone to Montreal up to three times between 1933 and 1935. The money she receives makes their life much easier. She breathes freely again. She pays her debts to Mr. Brûlé's grocery store and makes the house more comfortable. She has indoor plumbing installed and acquires a telephone.

SOCIAL LIFE

Since her return to Stanley Avenue, Marie-Louise's social life becomes a bit more active again. Her best friend is Mrs. Annie Sutherland.

Mother had one very good friend, Mrs. Sutherland, whose husband had left her. And she had three sons and she and mother would go out quite often. And for them, an outing was to go to the tea gardens on Sparks Street and to have their teacups read. They had a real mania for this. And she and Mother joined the bowling club at one time and she and Mrs. Sutherland would go, I think it was once a week. So that was about the biggest excitement that Mother had for quite a while.[43]

The power of the universe takes care of us and protects us. There are no coincidences. Mrs. Sutherland really is the best friend that Marie-Louise could have met. Both women were abandoned by their husbands. Both raise their children alone. They have a lot to share while sipping their tea. What do they say about men? Has Marie-Louise told her soul friend about her life with Joseph and the circumstances surrounding his departure, or has she kept the secret as promised? Annie Sutherland alone would have been able to tell us, but she has passed away.

Marie-Louise, who suffered so much from having been abandoned, sympathizes with people who live alone and never misses an opportunity to help them. This is revealed by the two following stories told to me by Gertrude.

> G: *We had an elderly neighbour, Mrs. Derby. She had pneumonia and lived all by herself. We went to get her on a sled and brought her home and Mother took care of her.*
> C: *She stayed at your house for a few days?*
> G: *Yes, for just a few days because I think she was then hospitalized.*[44]

And then:

> *She helped many neighbours, really. There was a woman who lived across the street. A Mrs. Slinn, I think. S-L-I-N-N. Dad had bought the property from these Slinns. She ended up going to the Pearly Home. It's on Aylmer Street in Ottawa. ... And I know that we went to visit her. She was an old woman and she didn't seem to have any family. ... [Mother] was a good woman. She tried to help, you know. And so naturally we all went.*[45]

Marie-Louise's interactions with her neighbours help fill the emotional void left when her husband abandoned her. For her, as for the children, the neighbours replace the relatives far away in Hanmer and in Blezard Valley.

> *And apart from that, she had some long-time neighbours, the Dawsons, who had been neighbours many years before Dad left. They had moved out and lived in the West End of the city. It was called Laurentian View in those days. It was near Britannia. And during the Holidays, one year we would go to their place for Christmas and they would come to our place for New Year's. Then the next year we switched [the invitations]. Anyway, they had four children about the same age as us. So we really liked to see them.*[46]

CONVALESCENT ᚻOME

After the humiliating trips to Montreal, Marie-Louise is more determined than ever to earn her living. With a nurse friend, Miss O'Neil, she maps out a project for a convalescent home where patients able to leave the hospital would come to complete their recovery before returning home. The idea is pretty innovative and the two women decide to go ahead with it. But they have no business knowledge at all and Marie-Louise can hardly read or write. Neophyte managers, they jump into this enterprise without knowing that they should have first conducted the equivalent of what is known today as a feasibility study. They hope that the Depression that closed so many businesses will spare theirs.

The project requires quite a considerable investment. They rent a home on Second Avenue in the Glebe, near the Canal. They buy furniture, beds and linens. To buy the basic necessities, Marie-Louise undoubtedly uses part of the money she received during her trips to Montreal and I imagine that her friend invests some of her savings too.

Marie-Louise leaves the children with a neighbour, Mrs. Jackson, who has no children and owns a cottage on Constance Bay. The children spend the summer there while Marie-Louise tries to start the convalescent home. But the project fails. I ask Gertrude:

> C: *Why did the project fail, do you know?*
> G: *I think that it is only because people didn't have money and I imagine that they kept their sick persons at home. In those days, for most people, that's the way it worked.*[47]

After about six months, Marie-Louise and her friend must face reality: they have lost all their investment!

KIOSK

Marie-Louise has to go back to square one. But she keeps her chin up.

She sells her car. She still has the house and the lots in her own name. While waiting to find another way to earn her living, she asks her neighbour, Albert Bennett, to build a small kiosk on the side of the house where she can sell candy and sodas. New investment. New failure. Gertrude explains:

> Hardly anyone lived nearby. There were only neighbours, so not enough people to sustain a market. ... And I think that there were more children eating the profits than anything.[48]

We laugh together. But sometimes when Gertrude thinks about her mother, it is with a feeling of admiration tinged with sadness, as revealed by her comment in the recording she handed to me: "Poor mother! She certainly tried a lot of things!"[49]

CHAPTER SIX

Living from Hand to Mouth

> So then we really started to experience
> hard times. Poor mother! Did she ever
> suffer a lot!
>
> ♂ GERTRUDE

JAMES STREET (1935–1936)

The Depression does not seem to loosen its grip on society, and like the majority of people, Marie-Louise cannot find work. The Stanley Avenue house is the sole source of revenue left. In 1935, short of money, she resigns herself to renting it out once more. An entrepreneur by the name of John W. Rostetter is interested. Marie-Louise does not rent the house fully furnished to him. She has rented a three-bedroom home at 187 James Street and takes her furnishings with her.

187 James Street

She moves in with her three children and Lorne's big dog. Following his Dad's departure, and the demise of Fairy, the four-legged garden guard, Lorne bought himself a dog, a part St. Bernard mutt. He paid for it with money saved from delivering newspapers. He loves his dog! He simply calls it Bernard.

He wasn't a pure Saint Bernard, but he was big. He was a good dog. And [Lorne] had built a sled for the dog to pull him around. Actually, we have photos of Lorne with his dog. Then in the summer he put wheels on the sled. He brought his "chums" along.[1]

Lorne, Marie-Louise's son, with his dog Bernard, circa 1934

Amply fed with oatmeal, bones and meat scraps given by the Billings Bridge butcher, Bernard has practically become a walking piece of furniture. So he is moved to the James Street house along with the rest of the furnishings.

On moving day, as Marie-Louise has no money to pay the movers, she gives them the piano. She counts on the payments that Mr. Rostetter will give her to pay for her rent on James Street. But he is also experiencing the impact of the Depression and can't get paid by his clients. He therefore cannot pay Marie-Louise who, through a ripple effect, cannot in turn pay her rent.

Circumstances lead me to believe that Marie-Louise once again calls on Joseph to get her out of trouble. First, on 19 August 1936,

Joseph sells one of the lots he had purchased in Capreol Township. It is Lot 8 of Concession II that he sells to Adélard Labre for the sum of $500 even though he had bought it for $670 in 1910. For what reason would he chose to sell this lot at a loss, in the middle of the Depression, apart from the fact that he has an urgent need for cash? We can think that it is to help out Marie-Louise since soon afterwards she seems to break her financial deadlock. Not only does she pay her rent, she decides once again to start a business.

LISGAR STREET (1936–1937)

Marie-Louise rents an imposing three-story, eight-bedroom home on Lisgar Street and transforms it in to a boarding house. The scope of this project supports the suggestion put forward earlier that she had received money from Joseph, otherwise where would she have found the funds necessary to furnish an eight-bedroom house? She certainly counts on her education *"in the art of tending a home and of being charming and loyal"*[2] to make her business a success. Furthermore, she had gained experience with the Second Avenue convalescent home.

Every move brings its sorrow and this one is no exception. Marie-Louise organizes the room distribution to maximize rental income. She puts her children on the third floor, Gertrude in one room and the boys in another. She rents the other two rooms on the third floor and the four rooms on the second floor. She sleeps on a couch in the dining room. Since they are so crowded, Lorne receives the order to get rid of his dog. Gertrude recalls:

> **G:** *I recall the day he went to put down his dog at*
> *the Humane Society. Oh, [he was] so heartbroken!*
> **C:** *He must have remembered it to his death.*
> **G:** *To his death.*[3]

Life resumes its course. Marie-Louise has pulled Gertrude out of the Rideau Street Convent and has enrolled her in Lisgar Collegiate. Lorne now works delivering telegrams and, through two of the boarders, Joe has found temporary construction work. In 1935, the government in order to create jobs has started the construction of the Bank of Canada building and the Post Office building on Besserer Street. Perhaps Joe is working there. But soon the work is completed and he finds himself unemployed again. The Depression keeps persisting and Marie-Louise cannot rent enough rooms to completely pay her rent. Once more, she lives from hand to mouth.

One day, Joe learns that they are hiring in the northern Ontario mines. He decides to go. Marie-Louise undoubtedly feels a pang at the idea of her 19-year-old son in the mines. She knows how hard this type of work is and she has not forgotten that her birth father died in a mining accident. The only consolation she has is that of knowing that he will stay at one of her cousin's. Joe hopes that the money he will send his mother will help solve her financial problems. But his departure doesn't solve anything. Before long, Marie-Louise cannot make ends meet. There is only one solution left.

On 2 January 1937, she mortgages the Stanley Avenue lots with Alfred Shaw as beneficiary. He lends her $500 and she commits to sending him regular payments. This money helps pay the arrears in her rent, but she still doesn't have enough boarders to fully pay her rent at the end of every month. In addition, Rostetter pays his Stanley Avenue rent very irregularly and never in full. The debt she just took on with Alfred Shaw only adds to the payments of her rent. Gradually, she sinks into a morass.

Meanwhile, the sisters at Rideau Street Convent worry about Gertrude's future.

> *I went to Lisgar High School until around Christmas.*
> *And then, the nuns at Rideau Street Convent thought*
> *that I would become a Protestant because I was going*

to Lisgar and that I was doomed. So they got in touch
with mother and I went back to the Convent for the
rest of the year, for free ... So, I think that the nuns
must have known the story.[4]

Maybe the nuns do know Marie-Louise's story. Gertrude is not the only adolescent at the Convent whose parents are having a hard time during the Depression. She knew a girl who lived in a tent with her family.

G: *I remember, when I went to the Convent, there*
was a girl whose parents had lost their home. So
there they were in Manor Park, camping with all
their furniture. ... So, you can imagine what kind
of life they had, right! But that was the Depression.
C: *Did they have a large family?*
G: *Well, I think there were quite a few of them.*
I don't recall. I do remember their name _____
because I knew the girl. But I don't remember how
it happened that I went to see where she lived ...
C: *You went there?*
G: *Yes, yes. And I couldn't believe it, you know. And*
in fact, all the furniture was there under a kind of
tent. ... It wasn't very big.[5]

Unfortunately, going back to Rideau Street Convent does not help Gertrude. In the two preceding years, she has experienced trying moves and she continues to feel the stress of watching her mother under pressure and of being powerless to help. Anxious about the family situation, she fails grade twelve.

And things just get worse. Soon, Marie-Louise receives eviction threats. As she knows full well that she won't be able to pay, she starts looking for another place to rent, in case the threats materialize. And at the beginning of the summer, the inevitable happens. Gertrude tells me:

> **G:** *Things were going really badly. She wasn't making enough money and a* bailiff *came. We were thrown out. And the* bailiff *sat on the porch to make sure we didn't take anything. He let us take only a table, some chairs and a bed each, you know.*
> **C:** *So what did she have to leave that he wouldn't let her take?*
> **G:** *Well, she had furnished the rooms to help out the boarders. There were beds, chests of drawers, and …*
> **C:** *And he wouldn't let you take any of that?*
> **G:** *No.*
> **C:** *Just the bare necessities for yourselves?*
> **G:** *Yes. She lost everything. It was total bankruptcy!*[6]

How destitute and totally abandoned Marie-Louise must feel there, on the sidewalk, with her daughter and her youngest son! And yet she does not lose her composure; she executes the Plan B that she had set up.

> **C:** *So what happened after that? You didn't know where to go that night?*
> **G:** *Well yes, we had rented a house on Nepean Street. Don't ask me where the money came from, I don't know. And so we moved there on Nepean Street with the pieces of furniture that he let us take.*[7]

NEPEAN STREET (1937–1939)

The house is located at 227 Nepean, just one street behind the house on Lisgar. It is a three-storey house. Marie-Louise sublets two of the rooms to secure a small income.

227 Napean Street today

I remember that a couple, a woman and her father,
had moved with us from the [Lisgar Street] house. …
They had two rooms there and when we moved to
Nepean Street they came with us. They were paying
[their rent] so I guess that helped.[8]

In spite of rent from these two rooms, Marie-Louise's financial situation is not improving. Mr. Rostetter is still not paying regularly.
Times are tough. Only the shrewdest people in business manage
to survive. If Mr. Rostetter has more than one creditor, he must
surely establish his priorities and take maximum advantage of the
flexibility he suspects he can get from one or another. Marie-Louise is not an aggressive person. Maybe it is easier to make her wait
to be paid than to make another more threatening person wait.
We can wonder why she doesn't terminate his lease and return to
her own home. Maybe she can't because the house is mortgaged.

Furthermore, she who is so inexperienced in business might be slightly intimidated by this educated businessman.

Soon, Marie-Louise finds herself gripped in a financial clutch and sees no way out of this situation. She must sell her house. On 3 May 1938 she sells the house and lots to John Rostetter for the amount of $4,000. According to the deed of sale, Rostetter assumes the remainder of the mortgage that Marie-Louise owes to Alfred Shaw. And since he doesn't have enough cash to buy the house and lots from Marie-Louise, he takes out a mortgage on them the same day for $3,480 with Marie-Louise as the beneficiary. From this moment on, he must make regular payments to Marie-Louise (probably on a monthly basis) until the sum has been paid in full with interest. With this sale, Marie-Louise is free from her debt to Alfred Shaw. But she receives no cash, except possibly a first monthly payment on the mortgage. The sale entails a great loss when one considers that Joseph paid $5,000 for the property in 1917 and that Marie-Louise has effected some renovations, such as installing indoor plumbing.

A few months later, in October, Gertrude leaves her mother to start her nursing studies in Cornwall.

> *I went to Cornwall because in those days you needed Grade 12 to go to the university and then to the General Hospital and I had not completed it. And the Civic Hospital was way too Protestant! I couldn't have gone to mass on Sundays.*

She gives me a mischievous look and I laugh.

> *As for the Sacré-Coeur in Hull, well I wasn't French-speaking enough. … So that is why I went to Cornwall. And, aside from that, in Cornwall, one of my girl friends was there taking the course.*[9]

RIDEAU STREET, CORNER OF CHAPEL (1939)

Gertrude's departure leaves Marie-Louise alone with her youngest son, Lorne, in the Nepean Street house. The country's economic situation is starting to slowly recover. The 1935 elections brought the Liberals back to power. They set up the National Employment Commission and, in 1937, created Trans-Canada Airlines, which would later become Air Canada. Finances are looking up and businessmen are starting to breathe easier. On 20 July 1939, John Rostetter pays Marie-Louise part of the mortgage — only for lot 133. This influx is still insufficient to pull Marie-Louise out of trouble. She and Lorne leave Nepean Street and move to a small apartment on Rideau Street at the corner of Chapel. Lorne becomes a day labourer.

Joseph Ray, eldest son of Marie-Louise and J.A. Roy

September 1, 1939, marks the beginning of the Second World War. Rumours are circulating. Some say that the Canadian government could eventually impose the conscription. Marie-Louise is probably worried since she has two bachelor sons. The War's momentum soon overtakes Canada. *"On September 10, [1939,] Canada declares war on Germany."*[10] The Government calls for men to enlist, and they respond in great numbers. Joe is 22 years old. He returns to Ottawa and submits a job application to the Royal Canadian Mounted Police. They accept him and send him to Regina for a training period. When he returns to Ottawa, he does not move in with Marie-Louise and Lorne.

Joseph Ray, eldest son of Marie-Louise and J.A. Roy

SLATER STREET (1940)

Marie-Louise and Lorne stay on Rideau Street for only a few months. Marie-Louise has at last found a job. She has been hired by the Government to clean offices. She and Lorne move to a bachelor apartment on Slater Street. The repeated moves she has been through and the bankruptcy have reduced her possessions to almost nothing.

I don't remember having anything to move. All we had was two beds. But still when we moved to Slater Street and we got there the apartment [we were to occupy] wasn't empty but the upstairs [apartment] was empty. We had to move in it and move down the next morning.[11]

Lorne laughs at the memory of this move, like one laughs afterwards about a sad story in the past. As with all bachelor apartments, the studio apartment on Slater Street has only one main room and a kitchen. Marie-Louise and Lorne make do pretty well. But in 1940 something unexpected changes their arrangement. Gertrude returns suddenly from Cornwall. She has contracted tuberculosis.

> *I was at my [nursing] course for one year when I contracted tuberculosis. That year, four of us caught it because we had had a patient from the Indian Reserve who was supposed to have pneumonia but it turned out to be tuberculosis.[12]*

In the early twentieth century, contracting tuberculosis was practically equivalent to a death sentence. No cures were known to combat it. It is only in the mid 1950s that a vaccine was developed. Gertrude is perfectly conscious of the danger she is in, not only because she is studying to be a nurse, but also because when they lived in Rideau Park she had known a girl who had tuberculosis.

> **G:** *I went to see her often. I sat on the porch with her and talked. She was only 20 years old. And then she died ... I was maybe only 15.*
> **C:** *Oh, my God! That must have been a shock for you to see a woman so young die of tuberculosis!*
> **G:** *Yes, yes. And then later I got it.*

C: *And when you got it, you must have remembered her.*
G: *For sure.*
C: *It must have come to your mind. You must have been afraid you might die because you saw her die, right?*
G: *Yes. I had seen her die ... yes, I knew.*[13]

The only thing that Marie-Louise can do to try and save Gertrude is to make her take to her bed for a total rest cure. Since the studio has only one bed — a Davenport sofa bed in the main room — Gertrude and her mother share it and Lorne sleeps on the kitchen floor in a sleeping bag. Gertrude remembers this long convalescence as the most boring time of her life.

G: *I had to stay LYING DOWN! All day! All the time! I only had permission to go to the toilet. That's all I was allowed to do ... I couldn't even knit!*
C: *No?*
G: *Because your arms, you know ... It had to be COMPLETE BED REST. Boring! It was really boring!*
C: *How long did this last?*
G: *For two years.*
C: *For two whole years? That's martyrdom!*
G: *Yes, I think I became mentally deficient during that time.*
[We burst out laughing together.]
C: *Could you at least read?*
G: *Yes, I could read. And Joe who was in the Mounted Police would bring me books from the Library. Boy, did I read!*[14]

Marie-Louise circa 1940

CENTRAL AVENUE (1941)

The following year, Marie-Louise, who now has a regular income thanks to her office cleaning job, decides to move to a more spacious abode with Gertrude and Lorne. She discovers a three-story house for sale at 5 Central Avenue. Since she has neither the means nor the intention to buy it, she rents with an option to purchase to lull the owner, who absolutely wants to sell. She then sub-lets the top half of the house to a couple.

But soon, the owner starts putting pressure regularly on Marie-Louise to finalize the purchase. Marie-Louise plays cat and mouse. She continues to imply that she intends to buy the property but avoids saying when she will do it. Eventually, the owner desists from pestering her, perhaps because the war does not facilitate house sales. The government has imposed restrictions on raising costs. *"… [A] freeze on salaries is decreed and this control also applies to rent and essential services like gas and electricity."* [15] It also sporadically imposes periods of blackout. *"For many minutes, street lights are extinguished, cars must circulate headlights off and houses, businesses, factories and stores must be plunged into darkness. The warning signal with its strident whistle sends a shiver of anxiety throughout the population."* [16]

Whatever the reasons for the house owner's change of mind, Marie-Louise ends up staying in the Central Avenue house for many years.

ACQUAINTANCE CHANGES (1942–1944)

The years 1942 to 1944 bring winds of change in Marie-Louise's acquaintances. New relations get established and old ones come undone. Like planets around a stable star, people circulate around her, sometimes closer, sometimes farther away.

First in 1942, thanks to her mother's tender care, Gertrude recovers her health and returns to Cornwall to complete her nursing studies, to her mother's great delight.

"She was so proud of me for returning!" [17] Gertrude tells me.

Marie-Louise resumes her life alone with Lorne. But soon it is the latter's turn to leave home. He is now 21 years old. He aspires to find a permanent job and the war offers him the opportunity to do so. He joins the Navy and is transferred to Halifax. As soon as he starts receiving a steady salary, he begins helping his sister financially.

In those days, Lorne was sending me "money orders"
for $10. Oh! That was a big gift! ... He sent some
to me several times ... in Cornwall. ... Lorne is an
angel! He really is an angel! [18]

Albert Laurent "Lorne" Ray, youngest son of Marie-Louise and J.A. Roy

Marie-Louise does not stay alone for long. Gertrude has a friend,
Alice Adam, who started her nursing degree with her in Cornwall.
Like Gertrude, Alice caught tuberculosis and had to interrupt her
studies. Always ready to help others, Marie-Louise gives her lodg-
ing for a while. Then after Alice's departure, she welcomes one
of her nieces, DesNeiges Bergeron, who comes from Hanmer to
work in Ottawa. DesNeiges spends all of 1942–43 with her. The
two women get along well. I ask DesNeiges about her stay with
Marie-Louise:

C: *What kind of outings did you do together? Would you go to the cinema?*

D: *Sometimes. Other times we just went for a walk to pass the time. She was very ... how do you say? She was very ordinary ... and extraordinary. ... She was a beautiful friend. ... She was very elegant.*

C: *Was she pretty?*

D: *Oh yes, and she knew it, too!*

C: *She fixed herself up well?*

D: *Aaah! You had to see her!* [19]

Even though Marie-Louise gets along well with her niece, she can be harsh with her when the latter tries to find out about her private life. This comes out by coincidence when I ask her:

C: *If I asked you three words to describe Marie-Louise, what would you say?*

D: *She was good, and she was gentle. She was nasty and "Get out of there, you."*

C: *When was she nasty?*

D: *When I had just pestered her.*

C: *OK. So if someone tried to get involved in her private life?*

D: *Her private life, it belonged to her.* [20]

December 3, 1942, marks the end of a business relationship. John Rostetter finally completes paying Marie-Louise the mortgage he signed on 22 April 1938. From that date onward, he has sole ownership of the Stanley Avenue house and lots.

Then the year 1943 blows a whirlwind of happy events through Marie-Louise's life. First, Joe, still in the RCMP, falls in love with a young woman named Marie Cécile Valois. Now, at that time there was a regulation in the Mounted Police according to which a man could not marry unless he had completed six years of service or he had special permission. But love proves to be stronger than regulations. On 1 July 1943, Joe and Cécile secretly marry at Christ Roy Church on Argyle Street, at 6 o'clock in the morning. Since Joe must continue to live in the Mounted Police barracks as if nothing had happened, Cécile returns to her parents' home where Joe visits her during his leave.

Marie-Louise at a picnic, circa 1943

Lorne has also met a woman that he likes. Her name is Isabella Hall and she is a native of Brockville. It doesn't take him long to follow Joe's example. On 8 October 1943, Marie-Louise has the great pleasure of attending their wedding. The newlyweds honeymoon in Halifax, where Lorne must complete his service in the Navy. After a few weeks, Isabella returns to her parents' home in Brockville. Lorne will join her at the end of the war and stay there until 1947.

Finally, a third event, this one slightly more comical, livens up Marie-Louise's life at the end of 1943. In December, Joe's wife Cécile becomes pregnant. The RCMP discovers the story of the secret marriage, thanks Joe for his services, and fines him $500 for having wed without permission. Marie-Louise does not miss seeing the funny side of the adventure and the good that comes with the bad. Joe and Cécile can finally live together openly. Marie-Louise puts them up on the second floor of the house on Central Avenue.

During 1944, Canada continues to manage the changes brought about by the war. In Ottawa, taxi and telephone services are still rationed. The Government does promulgate a law ensuring family allowances to parents who have children less than 16 years of age at home,[21] but these measures arrive too late to be of assistance to Marie-Louise. Her three children have reached adulthood. Anyway, she would not have dared to resort to it for fear of being asked questions.

As was 1943, the year 1944 brings a succession of significant events in Marie-Louise's life. First, at the beginning of the summer Gertrude completes her nursing studies. Marie-Louise feels immensely proud to see her daughter receive her diploma and get a job at the Ottawa General Hospital. She hastens to convince the new graduate to come live with her on Central Avenue.

A few months later, on 28 July, Joseph Ray (alias Jérémie Alphonse Roy) dies at L'Assomption. Does someone inform Marie-Louise of her "husband's" death? If so, she does not tell the children because Gertrude and Lorne tell me:

G: When father died in 1944, we didn't even know he was alive!

L: No. I wonder if mother knew.

G: No, I am sure she didn't. I don't think she heard from him at all. And I imagine that this was the agreement that they did when he left, that there would be no communication.[22]

Gertrude Ray, daughter of Marie-Louise and J.A. Roy, 1944

One thing is certain: the "widow" does not attend the funeral that took place on 31 July 1944, in Berthierville where he was born. On the death certificate, his name differs slightly from the one his birth certificate showed: D. Jérémie A. Roy. The "A" for Alphonse that he used during his mission out West has remained. As for the name "Joseph," it was buried along with the secret of his life with Marie-Louise.

It's seems like Nature hastens to fill voids. In families where a death occurs, often a birth arrives not long afterwards, and Marie-Louise's family offers another example of this. On 4 August 1944, Cécile, Joe's wife, gives birth to a little girl, Diane Ray. This happy event marks a new era in Marie-Louise's life. She is now a grand-mother.

CHAPTER SEVEN

1944 TO *1965*

Nanny

> *We called her Nanny. I think that that says everything ...*
>
> ❧ PATRICK MANTHA

GRANDMOTHER

Marie-Louise is simply delighted to be a grandmother. And God knows she will have this pleasure many times over. Between 1944 and 1960, twelve more grandchildren are added to the first grand-daughter. For each one of them, she becomes a memorable presence, someone to whom they will remain attached all of their lives.

On 21 September 1946, Gertrude weds Paul-Emile Mantha. Marie-Louise is 55 years old. All three of her children are now married. She can relax, knowing that she is no longer responsible for their well-being, that all three have loving spouses and that they are quite able to face their own future. She now enters a phase of life where she can devote all the time she desires to her role as a grandmother.

Gertrude Ray's wedding, 21 September 1946.
Marie-Louise is at the end on the right.

Her grandchildren called her and still call her Nanny. When I ask them in turn what impressions come to mind about their grandmother, they all speak of her with love and admiration, and in the most touching terms. From these interviews I glean the portrait of a patient and gentle grandmother who adores them, who does not hesitate to hug them close to her heart and who represents for them *"warmth, comfort and protection."* [1] A grandmother always in a good mood, who gives generously of herself by working non-stop for them and by taking the time to make small gifts by hand for their parties and birthdays. A woman always well groomed, a "class act," [2] who enjoys simple pleasures and whose sensitivity masks a will of iron. Lastly, a woman who's silence, sometimes sad, gives off a glimpse of her profound depth, hard for the children to grasp. One of her granddaughters sums up her portrait with a heart-felt phrase, *"For me, Nanny was boundless love."* [3]

There is no doubt that Marie-Louise intends doing all she can as a grandmother to shower affection on her grandchildren and to help give them what she couldn't give to her own children after Joseph's departure: a childhood and an adolescence free of all material and emotional worry. She bestows her unconditional love on them and devotes all her talents to expressing it.

SEWING AND KNITTING

Nimble fingers. That's what they are, these fingers that produce dresses, coats, trousers, blouses and underpants. To help out her daughter and daughters-in-law, Marie-Louise makes most of her grandchildren's clothes, for the boys as well as for the girls.

> She made us many, many outfits: tiny coats with matching hats. And when I got married, Nanny and my Mom made their own dresses, my wedding dress, my going away dress, and dresses for Anne, Pauline and Suzanne. She worked and worked! [4]

She sews all these clothes on a simple foot-pedal sewing machine, probably bought through the Eaton's catalogue. Later, her son Lorne will add a motor to make it easier for her and prevent her from getting leg cramps. She oversees her grandchildren's wardrobes with all the experience she learned during the lean years. Nothing is wasted! From items that no longer fit one child, she fabricates wonders for another.

> She would take a coat from Lorne's wife who didn't want it anymore and make a coat for me. ... I remember one I loved. It was a little coat. It had fur on the cuffs and she made me a little fur muff. I LOVED it! And I felt so special in it.[5]

She uses her imagination and creativity to exploit in the most unexpected ways any cloth she can get her hands on, even material not usually destined for sewing clothes:

> *Papa had bought some parachute cloth from the Army Surplus in Toronto. She took that material and made us blouses and underpants, ... in this heavy, white nylon, you know. It could resist anything![6]*

And with the same material she confects a toy for her grandson:

> My Dad had a real parachute and she took a piece of the cloth and made me a parachute with it so I could throw it up in the air.[7]

What's more, she doesn't just sew for the children. She also sews for their dolls.

> *Every Christmas, we got a new dress and our doll did, too. You see. Everything matched. They were always chosen with care, beautifully decorated with lace where it was needed.[8]*

Gertrude tells me:

> *She made doll clothes for all my children. And GOR-*
> *GEOUS things! Do you remember Mary Poppins?*
> *She dressed a doll for Suzanne and Pauline as Mary*
> *Poppins. And it was so well done! It was beautiful!*
> *[My daughters] were the only ones in the neighbour-*
> *hood to have nice clothes like that to play Mary Pop-*
> *pins. They could dress it and undress it.*[9]

Marie-Louise sews jeans for the boys, and knits mittens, tuques, scarves and wool socks for them.

> I remember also she knitted me a hat. It was a tuque
> that I just hated! It was one with the thing that goes
> down underneath and I didn't want to offend her.
> So I would wear it as I went out of the house and
> then as soon as I got down the street, I would take
> it off. … It was red and blue.[10]

IN THE KITCHEN

Nanny shares her cooking talents with her loved ones. The grand-children remember:

> *She made very good soups. … She made a Scottish soup,*
> *what she called a* Scotch broth. *That was, I remem-*
> *ber, one of her best soups. And my father always said*
> *that nobody could cook a roast like my grandmother:*
> *roast pork or roast beef.*[11]
> *She loved tea, not coffee. And she adored lamb. …*
> *She had habits more … English I would say. It wasn't*
> *lamb.* It was mutton *because that it was they had*

known, I guess, during the Depression and during the war, mutton with mint jelly, *you know.*[12]

David, Lorne's son, recalls a rather frugal grandmother who sometimes prepared a salad with dandelion leaves that made him wince a little bit.

Potatoes make up an incontrovertible part of Nanny's cuisine. It is the first thing she puts on the stove when preparing a meal and she makes them with every meal which sometimes bothers Gertrude's husband, who does not necessarily desire to eat potatoes every single day.

But what we love can become our downfall in the hands of an enemy. Cathy (S) Lorne's daughter, tells me:

> **S:** She always had meals with us and she always washed the dishes every night and she LOVED her mashed potatoes. Every night she would have to have potatoes.
>
> **C:** Always mashed?
>
> **S:** Always mashed. Oh! I should say mashed or boiled potatoes but nothing any fancier than that. And yeah, to her a meal was not complete if there weren't potatoes involved. And I always knew if … like her and my mum, they got along fine. But I mean of course, you know, you've got two cooks in the kitchen, sometimes there would be squabbles. We were not a very vocal household, so there would not be any screaming, but I always knew when she and my mum were in a tiff because my mum wouldn't make potatoes. … My mum wouldn't make potatoes and Nanny wouldn't wash the dishes and I would know: that's it! They were not speaking to each other. But then the next day, it all seemed to be back to normal.[13]

Marie-Louise (Nanny) and her granddaughter Diane, circa 1945

"BREAKING CAMP"

In 1947, Gertrude and Paul-Emile move into a nice, large home that they had built in Orleans. They rent the upstairs to Joe and Cécile. Since the latter free up the second floor on Central Avenue, Marie-Louise invites Lorne and Isabella to leave Brockville and to come live with her. They accept.

Then in 1949, new moving around! Paul-Emile accepts a job with the Ontario Government in Toronto. He sells the Orleans home and goes to Toronto on his own first to find housing for his family. Gertrude and her two babies, Louise and Anne, move to Central Avenue with Marie-Louise for a few months, and then they leave to join Paul-Emile.

As for Lorne and Isabella, they buy a house in Ottawa south, on Fentiman Avenue. They invite Marie-Louise to come live with them. This proposal offers advantages to Marie-Louise. She would not have the bother of finding boarders anymore for the second floor on Central Avenue. She would no longer have to pay rent, and, more importantly, she could share precious moments with her grandson, David. She accepts.

The move is somewhat painful for her, because she has to "break camp." She can't bring all her possessions to Lorne's. In preparing to move, Lorne and Isabella sort out what they can bring to the new home and leave on the front lawn the things that they relegate to the garbage. While they are busy in the house, Marie-Louise pulls out of the garbage things she can't bear to part with and brings them back into the house through the back door. This game of "in one door, out the other" ends when Lorne and Isabella realize that they have taken out the same things more than once. Through negotiations, they arrive at an understanding.

MOTHER-IN-LAW

Marie-Louise adapts well to the house on Fentiman Avenue except for a small detail that Lorne laughingly describes to me, "I remember her being sea-sick on the veranda rocking the chair." [14]

If Marie-Louise is nauseous, it may be because while rocking, she is reflecting on the consequences that will follow the change of direction her life just took. For the first time since she left Hanmer, she doesn't have her own home. She now lives with her son and daughter-in-law. She cannot make decisions anymore concerning the organization of her own environment. She must consult her daughter–in-law about all initiatives concerning the management of the household. In this new context, her status as mother-in-law is linked like a shadow to her status as grandmother. And she cannot separate from it as Peter Pan separated from his shadow. She must keep that in mind while carving alongside her daughter-in-law a support role that is as efficient and discreet as possible. What an apprenticeship for a woman who has run her own ship freely all these years without asking anyone's approval!

She looks after her grandson, helps with the chores, and takes part in the meal preparation. But she prefers sewing in her room so as not to constantly impose her presence.

In 1950 Gertrude and her husband invite her to come and live with them in Toronto and she accepts with pleasure. She is 59 years old and the idea of leaving her job with the Government to go live in a new city appeals to her.

As she did at Lorne's, she lends her daughter a hand and tries to impose herself as little as possible. Gertrude's husband, Paul-Emile, is a tolerant man and he loves his mother-in-law. But, whether one likes it or not, it is always difficult to live with one's mother-in-law, even if she is the nicest person in the world. So, inevitably, tensions flare up from time to time.

> *There was some tension in the house because, and I understand it now, for my father it wasn't pleasant to have his mother-in-law there all the time ... If my parents had friends over, well she sat there in the living room, too ... It's sad to say, but she was there like an intruder. ... There was tension between my parents because she was always there. ... I know that Dad said things sometimes. ... He loved her! But, you know, when you have someone visiting you all the time, all the time, all the time. And besides that, it's your mother-in-law! ... She wasn't the type of obtrusive mother-in-law. She didn't impose herself at all. She was in the background but she was there.*[15]

In fact, she imposes herself so little that she is "*like a mouse*"[16] in the house. She is quite aware that her constant presence causes tension. She finds ways to absent herself from time to time to give the young couple a bit of privacy. She stays in her room to sew and goes out sometimes with her friend Betty Fleming, a Toronto woman who has seven children. The memories that Betty will write down later on in a note to Gertrude reveal the empathy that Marie-Louise feels for women in difficult situations and her subtlety at finding discreet ways to help.

Madame Rae: a very sweet sociable little lady who enjoyed doing nice things for friends, i.e. making a parachute silk dress for one of my infants, baby-sitting while I was in hospital having another baby and on many occasions to let me and my husband "get away." Also, on occasion, she could come up with a good one-liner. She was a doting grand-mother, mother of her three, and positively glowed with pride over them all.[17]

Nanny in Toronto with her Mantha grandchildren, circa 1954

JAKE AND THE KID

On occasion, Marie-Louise returns to Ottawa to spend time at one or the other of her sons' home. Lorne bought a house in August 1950 on Larose Avenue and Marie-Louise comes for short stays from time to time. Her grandson, David, remembers happy moments spent with her:

She was a great grandmother! I mean, you know, she looked like a grandmother and was always there for you. When I was in grade one and two, my mother always worked, so she would give me lunch and I guess one of my strongest recollections with her is going home for lunch. And we always used to listen to *Jake and the Kid*. It was on at noon hour.[18]

Marie-Louise loves to please her grandson and this program gives her the opportunity to do so, since *Jake and the Kid* tells about the adventures of a young boy in the Canadian Prairies in the early twentieth century. The series of 320 episodes written by Ormond Mitchell was broadcast on radio between 1949 and 1957.

Marie-Louise in Toronto, circa 1952

GOD

In March 1951, when Cécile, Joe's wife, gives birth to her third child, Michael, Marie-Louise comes again to Lorne's home and brings over Donald, the little 4-year-old, for a few days while his mother is in the hospital. Donald recalls:

There was one time that I was staying with Nanny Ray at my uncle's home while my mother was in the hospital giving birth. At the time, I didn't understand what my mother was going through, but in my mind, I felt that she was in grave danger. Nanny could see my concern and talked to me about it. I was still very concerned so she suggested that I walk up to the local church and say a prayer for my mum. I did that, and remember being in the church ALL ALONE "talking to God." After I had verbalized my request sufficiently, I returned to Nanny and told her about my experience. She assured me that now that a child had made a request to God, that everything would be fine. Therefore, when the birthing went without incident (at least that was what I was told), I was not surprised and felt that I had played a big part in the outcome.[19]

It is interesting to note that Marie-Louise encourages her grandson to "dialogue" with God. After what she lived through, one could expect her faith to be strongly shaken, but it seems not, as revealed in my conversation with her oldest granddaughter:

> **D:** I remember having an argument with her about God. I said to her that there is no God. And she said, "YES, THERE IS!" And it would be like, "No, there isn't." "Yes, there is!" You know. "No, there isn't." And we argued. I was an adult, a young adult. And I said, "Okay, Nanny. If you die before me and there is a God, you come back and tell me."
> **C:** What did she say?
> **D:** She said, "I will!" And that was it.[20]

All her grandchildren remember her as a woman of faith. She goes to Mass by choice and not because she is under obligation. She kneels down by her bedside to say her prayers and says her rosary regularly. But she considers her spiritual life a private affair and does not impose on others to pray or to go to church with her.

BACK TO OTTAWA (1957–1965)

In 1957, the Mantha family moves back to Ottawa, and settles at 38 Sweetland Avenue in Sandy Hill. As three more children were born in Toronto, the house is not big enough to accommodate Marie-Louise. She therefore moves to Lorne's home on Larose Avenue. She will reside there until 1970.

She frequently visits Gertrude to help out and takes this opportunity to do activities with the children.

> *I remember taking the bus with her to go stay overnight at my cousin Cathy's, where Nanny was living at the time. I recall that she curled our hair, you know, and she played with us like we were dolls.*[21]

OGILVY'S

But Nanny's most frequent outings with her grandchildren are her shopping trips to Ogilvy's department store on Rideau Street. It is her favourite store.

> *I remember going shopping at Ogilvy's with her. We went to the bathroom because she would hide her money in her corset, … in her girdle. … So we had to go to the bathroom so she could take out her money to be able to go shopping.*[22]

She buys all her sewing materials there. Since she shops there quite frequently, she knows all the clerks in the sewing section and introduces her grandchildren to them with great pride. Once the purchases are completed, they go down to eat at the cafeteria in the basement, a very special treat for the children.

She does the same thing with her niece Georgette when she comes from Hanmer to visit her. Georgette emphasizes the fact that Nanny wore gloves to go shopping as dictated by the etiquette of the day.

CINEMA

Another pleasure that Nanny delights in sharing with her grandchildren is going to the cinema. Her passion for films has never diminished since the presentation in Ottawa of the first talking film, *The Jazz Singer* with Al Jolson, in 1927. As soon as the grandchildren reach the age where they can sit still for over an hour, she keeps an eye on the cinema schedule at the Nelson Theatre and carefully chooses something of appeal for each grandchild: Walt Disney's *Bambi* for one granddaughter, *Fiddler on the Roof* for a grandson. In 1963, a film by Alfred Hitchcock comes out, which soon gets the reputation of being very frightening. Nanny takes Anne, who is 14 years old.

> *I remember that she took me to see* The Birds *by Alfred Hitchcock ... I was so afraid that she would have a heart attack!*[23]

THE COUNTESS OF *SÉGUR*

Some stories the grandchildren tell me about Nanny remind me of the Countess of Ségur,[24] who like Nanny was always telling her grandchildren to be kind and good, and whose stories always contained a lesson to be learned. Two stories in particular describe a

"Nanny–educator" who doesn't miss a chance to transmit a small message. The first one was told to me by her eldest granddaughter, Diane:

> There was another time when she got mad at me. It was quite a lesson that I learned from her. I didn't mean to be bad. Again, I don't remember how old I was. But we were in the Aylmer house. And it was Christmas and my parents used to give us money to buy Granny a present, right? And I was trying to get everyone a present and I forgot that I hadn't got a present for Nanny. And I had no money and I knew I couldn't get anymore. So I rummaged through my drawer and found this bottle of perfume that I had never opened. It had been a gift. I don't know if I remember who gave it to me. So I wrapped it up very pretty and put it under the tree for Nanny. And I didn't think anything of it, you know after that. I don't remember anything about that Christmas. But the following Christmas, I got that perfume back from Nanny. And I was so disappointed because she always gave us something that she would make for Christmas. And I couldn't wait to open my present. And I sat there and thought about it. And I thought, "This is the present I got her." And then I thought, "Oh God! She gave me that! " And then I looked at her and she was like this. [She imitates her grandmother staring at her.] Oh! I was upset at her and she was upset at me. And we never spoke about it. And I never told my parents. Actually, I don't think I have ever told anyone. But it was something I remembered.[25]

The second story divulges Nanny's generous heart and her clever way of giving a lesson in charity to her grandchildren. The story takes place one day when the children caught head-lice in school and they had to stay home so as not to spread the affliction.

> *Jean-Pierre, Pauline and I had caught head-lice. We lived on Sweetland Avenue at the time. We were very young. We had a neighbour who was named* _____ *and he came to ask if we could go out to play. And we yelled out from the window that we had lice. Nanny was babysitting us then. Since we couldn't go out, he went behind our house where there was a shed and, right in front of our eyes, took the wooden dollhouse that stayed outdoors. And Nanny refused to stop him from leaving with it. ... She said to me, "Let him take it. He might need it more than you." And. ... of course he was quite poor. But I remember being so shocked that she let him go. ... My dollhouse!*[26]

Nanny who has known moments of abject poverty silently understands the uncontrollable urge to steal that a poor child might experience in front of a nice toy. Indulgent, she tries to give her grandchildren a lesson in charity by telling them to let him go.

The children learn other lessons watching their grandmother live her daily life. Marie-Louise's grandson, Patrick, writes to me:

> *If anyone in the world taught me to understand the word* frugal, *it is definitely my grandmother. ... She knew how to survive and how to "cut a penny in four." She never wasted a piece of string or a sewing pin. Table scraps, either. She searched and bargained to her satisfaction, sometimes coming up empty-handed, not*

having found what she wanted. Sometimes it was ex-
asperating for the young boy I was, tugging at her skirt
hem. But, oh, how examplary and educational![27]

A BUSY ROOM (1962–1965)

In 1962, the Mantha family moves to 29 Sweetland Avenue. Since
the house is bigger, a room is set up for Nanny to sleep over when
she wants to. Although she still lives with Lorne, Nanny stays intermittently at Gertrude's.

The room she occupies at 29 Sweetland has the distinctive fea-
ture that one must pass through it to get to the attic where the boys
have their bedroom. So sometimes it happens that the boys pass
through her room just as she is getting dressed. They discover with
a tinge of curiosity and discomfort that Nanny wears a whalebone
corset fastened with ties. Nanny is now over 70 years old and surely
doesn't appreciate having impromptu visitors in her most private
moments. If she desires a place all of her own, where she could re-
tire with the certainty of not being disturbed, she doesn't say so to
Gertrude and her husband because she knows very well that they
can do nothing about it.

THE SECRET

Although Nanny maintains a very close relationship with her grandchildren, who see her regularly, they have a feeling that a part of
her remains inaccessible to them. David recounts:

> I recollect of her too standing at the back win-
> dow and talking to herself. ... She was talking in
> French so I couldn't understand her but I remem-
> ber walking in the room and she was looking at the
> window very calm and she suddenly knew that I

was there and she was not embarrassed at all. So
... but what she was talking about or who she was
talking to ....[28]

What is Marie-Louise thinking about as she looks out the window?
Who is she talking to like that in French? Is she telling someone
about the events of the day, about the emotions that she is feeling
and that she cannot share with anyone?

David is not the only one of the grandchildren to sense an enigma
in his grandmother. During the same period of time, in Toronto,
her granddaughter Louise notes:

> *There was a deep sadness that I felt emanating from*
> *her. There was a very sad underpinning.*[29]

Similarly, Suzanne, Louise's sister, felt that her grandmother kept
a secret about her grandfather and that her efforts to try and find
out the nature of that secret only opened a painful wound:

> *I felt uncomfortable with her because every time I tried*
> *to find out about my grandfather she often changed the*
> *story and then she started to cry. And so I just avoided*
> *raising the topic.*[30]

When I ask Cathy (S), David's sister, for three words to describe
her grandmother, she answers:

S: I would say she was fun loving, but at the same
time, mysterious. And cuddly. She was very cuddly.
C: Now why mysterious?
S: I guess just because the tears I would see
sometimes, ... cause she spent a lot of time
alone and seemed to like it that way. ... So just

introspective all the time, you know. She had
a lot on her mind and maybe sort of mumbling
away to herself sometimes and I wondered what
she was thinking about. And later on when I
found out about her history and how tough
things had been, it all made such perfect sense.
At the time, the little quirks that I thought
that she had, like the crying and just the quiet
behaviour at times, when other times she could
be so outgoing. It all made sense.

C: Your brother told me that, one day, he caught
her near the window, talking to herself quietly.
Did it happen to you too?

S: Often! Yes. She would be like that. She would
just kind of be staring off and sort of mumbling.
I would look at her and wonder what it is that
she would be talking about.

C: Was she talking in French or in English?

S: In French. It was usually in French.

Cathy does not speak French. She therefore doesn't understand a
word of her grandmother's veiled soliloquy.

That's what occurred to me, that she was praying
or just trying to sort through things on why her life
had turned out the way it had or taken the course
of events. But I don't think she felt sadness. I certainly never sensed bitterness in her, EVER. But
there was maybe a sadness there that things had
turned out ... would have wished that things have
turned out differently. But NEVER angry. Or never
feeling like a victim.[31]

It is certain that Marie-Louise keeps inside her heart a Pandora's box in which she conceals her memories, her feelings and the thoughts that she could never express. This is what makes her pensive sometimes. She hides from her grandchildren her love story with Joseph and his return to the priesthood. She keeps the promise made to him of never revealing it to anyone. She does not want to open the box on any pretext, for fear of seeing her memories escape, change with the re-telling or be sullied by gossipmongers. And even if her daughter is now a mother and women often share intimate secrets amongst themselves, she keeps the silence into which she locked herself up all these years. I ask Gertrude:

C: *When she spent afternoons with you, did she talk about her life a little?*
G: *Never, never! It was a big, big secret.*

In spite of the years that have passed, Marie-Louise maybe still feels the need to pour her heart out, to tell her children about the wonderful love she and Joseph lived before their arrival, and to clarify once and for all the mystery surrounding his departure. But what good would it do? What is the use of telling them how and why their father returned to the priesthood? What is the use of telling them that their real name is Roy and not Ray? Why upset their lives?

Really, when you think about it, that she kept it secret for so long, it must have been terrible![32]

CHAPTER EIGHT

1960 TO 1964

Return to Her Roots

GRADUATION (1960)

As adults, salmon follow their instincts and swim up the river where they were born to lay their eggs. Similarly, birds return to their place of birth to build a nest for their young. It is nature's cycle and human beings can't escape it. With old age comes the desire to see our childhood places, the house where we grew up and the people who shared our childhood games, our adventures and our dreams for the future.

In 1960, an event triggers Marie-Louise's return to her roots. Her godchild in Hanmer, Georgette Bergeron, has just completed her nursing degree, and invites her to the graduation ceremony.

> *When I graduated from nursing in* 1960, *my mother* [*Claire-Hilda*] *had had a heart attack and was in the hospital. She couldn't come to the graduation so I asked my aunt to come. It is she who represented my mother at the convocation.*[1]

Georgette Bergeron's graduation, 1960.
Marie-Louise is to the right of the graduate.

A lot of water has passed under the bridge since Marie-Louise's reunion with her family after Joseph's departure. Her adoptive father, Napoléon, died in 1950, her children are married, she has lived in Toronto and she has become a grandmother. Marie-Louise is now 69 years old. The sister she loves so much is in the hospital and she realizes that she might have lost her. Is it for this reason that she feels more deeply than before the need to spend time in her childhood haunts, to see once more the members of her extended family and to chat at length with them?

Marie-Louise and her godchild Georgette Bergeron, 1960

THE TWO GOSSIPS

In the years following this visit to Hanmer, the bond between Marie-Louise and her sister becomes even tighter. Claire and her girls come to visit her in Ottawa every year and Marie-Louise returns frequently to spend a month with them. Georgette relates:

We would say, "Aunty would you like to come to Sud-
bury?" Ah! The night before, her bags were packed.
"Are you coming?" "Oh, yes, I've decided to come."
Well, then it was a race to find her medication so
that she would have enough for almost a month. And
then the whole time she was here, my mother and her
laughed! They laughed for thirty days![2]

The three sisters (left to right):
Dorilla and the "two gossips," Claire and Marie-Louise

This month per year with her sister, far from the city, allowed Marie-Louise to revitalize herself. The two women would relax and
act frivolously.

They would go to the cabin in the woods. No electric-
ity, no running water. And, before my aunt arrived,
one of us, Georgette or me, would purchase at the li-
quor store a case of Porter for the two of them. … And
my father [Florian] sat outside to smoke in his rocking
chair. They each had a rocking chair and before din-
ner they would have a little drink of Porter.

And my father would say, "I'm sitting here, and
they giggle all day." [3]

Florian can't get over seeing Claire-Hilda and Marie-Louise chat
and laugh for hours. He has nicknamed them *"the two gossips."*

INNER PEACE

During her trips to Hanmer, Marie-Louise stays close to her family. She seldom goes out and does not attempt to re-establish contact with neighbours and friends from her youth. However one
day, she takes an unexpected initiative.

> *Once she came up and seemed to want to talk. So she*
> *said "I'm going to go visit Miss Albina Beaulieu." Al-*
> *bina Beaulieu lived on the farm next door. She was*
> *Louis' daughter. Louis and Napoléon had arrived here*
> *at the same time, and brought up their families [at the*
> *same time]. So Marie-Louise went off to see Albina. ...*
> *She was there for many hours. And when she returned,*
> *my mother said, "She was radiant!" She seemed happy*
> *as if a load had been lifted from her shoulders.* [4]

It had taken courage for Marie-Louise to visit Albina. Given her
irregular marital situation and the distance she kept for years from
the people of Hanmer, she had no idea how she would be received.
What did the two women talk about? What childhood memories
or difficulties in their respective lives did they reminisced together?
Only God knows. But it seems as if Albina received her with open
arms because Marie-Louise came back home beaming with new
confidence. Having renewed her friendship with Albina gives her
the feeling of having symbolically won Hanmer back. She feels
free! She feels that she just knocked down within herself the last

obstacle that was stopping her from confronting public opinion. Georgette describes to me the "new" Marie-Louise:

> *I know that in the 1960's, ... the first years, she did not like to go places. After she spoke with Albina, it was as if she carried her head higher, and she would go out with us, and we would go to places and it seems like, "Huh! I'm here, I know who I am. The rest of you, do you know who you are?" ... And after that she did not seem to mind going out.*[5]

Marie-Louise (Nanny) and her grandchildren David and Cathy Ray, July 1964

In fact, she now enjoys going out. The appetite from her youth for meeting new people and exploring unknown territories reawakens in her soul and she knows that, from now on, others' opinions will not prevent her from living life as she sees fit.

THE TRIP TO THE YUKON

In September 1964, Marie-Louise again visits her sister Claire-Hilda in Hanmer. As usual, the two gossips start scheming and this time they don't content themselves with talk, they take action. They intend to go to the Yukon.

The Yukon! Land of the midnight sun! The very name of this

territory evokes for every Canadian the Klondike and the Gold Rush at the end of the nineteenth century. It stirs up in memories images of the sea of humans lured by instant riches. This name, so unique, conveys legends about gold discoveries of mythical proportions.

Florian, Claire-Hilda's husband, and both girls, Clothilde and Georgette, adopt the idea with enthusiasm.

> So we said, "We're going to the Yukon." In fact, we have a cousin of the two gossips that went to the Yukon during the gold rush and he never came back. We never knew him, but the adventure of going to see where he went. So they said, "Well then, let's get ready and go."[6]

Marie-Louise and Claire-Hilda are in charge of the meals. Since the travellers expect to be gone for a whole month, the two women prepare preserves to eat at noon along the way. They set off at noon on a Saturday.

> We [thought] we would get perhaps to Sault Ste Marie, it was about four hours. We only got to Thessalon, I think, one hour outside the Sault, maybe half an hour. We stayed in a motel. The cabins were on Georgian Bay, on the shores of Lake Huron. We spent the night there. The next morning, we went to Mass in Thessalon and then we left.

Florian is very frustrated because the women won't let him smoke in the car. They are travelling in a fairly big automobile, a sedan. Clothilde and Georgette are the two appointed drivers. Every two hours they switch roles and this gives everyone time to get out of the car and move a little. Florian takes the opportunity to smoke his pipe.

At noon we would stop; [the two gossips] got out the grub and we played ball. And then we left again and stopped to sleep. We always had to find a motel with a kitchenette because we had to cook dinner. If there was no kitchenette, we had to get our stove out of the car. … So we went to the Yukon with little trips here and there. I think we stopped in Regina to see Lorne's son, David … It was an extraordinary trip. … We went to Vancouver to see our cousin. Then we crossed to Victoria to see the Butchart Gardens and what there is to be seen in Victoria. After that, we went to the Yukon. We drove up and it took three, maybe four days.

They drive to Dawson where they can find no traces whatsoever of the mythical cousin who never returned from the Gold Rush. But who cares! They have seen the Yukon and start to head for home, happy to have set foot in this historical part of the world.

The funniest story of the trip occurred on our way back, in the interior of B.C. when we stopped at Chetwynd, near Willston Lake. There are a lot of ranches around there. It was cattle drive time. We found a motel with a small room and a kitchenette. … So [one of the gossips] said, "We'll go to the store and get fresh steaks and veggies and salad fixings." So [Georgette and I] went to the store and as we left we went to the hotel because you could buy beer in hotels. We would buy six or seven pints to have some for tomorrow night. Then we went back to the motel and made supper. After supper, we said, "Do you want to come and see? The cowboys are all at the hotel." And my father answered, "Well I'm not interested." So the two gossips got dressed and off we went …
We walked into the hotel and the man seated us.

*And of course, all the men there, some were Mexican
and some were American, they were all cowboys and it
was a Saturday night.*

Clothilde and I laugh together imagining the four women concerned
with proprieties, while seated at a table in a room full of happy,
slightly tipsy cowboys who, leaning on the bar, look at them with
lustful eyes and take the liberty of making slightly bawdy jokes.

*So they started talking with us. They sent over a few
beers for my sister and me. Then they sent gin to our
mothers. I think our mothers were drinking gin. Then
they started to auction off the two women (Marie-
Louise and Claire-Hilda).*

Marie-Louise is 73 years old and Claire-Hilda is 66. They are
amused and slightly flattered in spite of themselves to be getting
this attention. They let the game go on.

*Yes, they auctioned off the two women. At the end
my aunt won. It was a young bucko [who won] and
he sent her a drink. That was the game. And it was
funny because they were not insulting and they were
having as much fun as we were.*

So the return trip proceeds. They pass through Calgary again to
visit a cousin, Melva, the daughter of Paul Labelle (Napoléon ju-
nior]), Marie-Louise's brother. From Regina onwards, they travel
in pouring rain, which does not deter them from completing the
round of cousins before returning home. They take Highway 11
going north, pass by Nipigon and go all the way to Kapuskasing
where another cousin lives.

I wasn't really watching the clock. The first thing I know, it is one o'clock in the morning when we arrive at the cousin's house. He was a cousin on my grandfather's side. And he had seven children.

I can only imagine the cousin's astonishment to see five people land in unannounced at one o'clock in the morning. He wakes up his wife, "Darling, we've got company."

So we slept there! The next day, we went to Cochrane to visit the father of my mother's cousin, my uncle Louis. So we saw Louis and spent a day there. ... Then we returned to Sudbury.

We were gone a month. Three weeks and five days, something like that. We travelled many miles, saw a lot of country, and had a lot of fun. Do you know that we don't have any photos? Not one from the Yukon.

No photos, but certainly a wealth of pleasant memories in Marie-Louise's mind.

CHAPTER NINE

1965 TO *1970*

Old Age, Humour and Tenderness

> "The house with an old grandparent
> harbours a jewel."
>
> ✧ CHINESE PROVERB

159

A TIME TO RELAX

In 1965, the Mantha family moves again, this time to a large three-story duplex on Stewart Street at the corner of Charlotte. They rent one side and move into the other. Nanny is still living with Lorne on Larose Avenue and comes to visit them often, just as she did on Sweetland Avenue. The grandchildren are now adolescents, except for Lorne's youngest, Cathy, who is only 6 years old. They are more independent and their activities gravitate around their friends.

Since Nanny has a little more time for herself, she joins the Good Companions, an organization for senior citizens.

> It's a senior citizens club kind of thing ... and it was down on Bronson, just across from where the new War Museum is. ... This was a community centre that she belonged to and maybe once a week she would go down there and they would play cards and just, you know, socialize. And every year they would have a grandchild day and she would bring me down to grandchild day and just see all of these seniors just glowing, you know, just so happy to have their grandchildren.[1]

Orange earthen pot, circa 1972

She explores several artistic activities at the Good Companions' Club. Her grandchildren still have some of the objects that she made there, among them an earthen pot and an engraved metal plate.

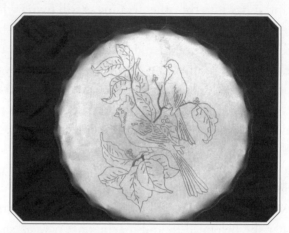

Engraved metal plate

At Lorne's house, she spends a lot of time with her granddaughter Cathy (S):

> S: She didn't go out much at all. Except for these trips to the Good Companions, she rarely went out. So she and I spent a lot of time together.
> C: What would you do?
> S: We would watch TV and ... well, she painted a lot too.

Marie-Louise has come back to her first love. From the silk painting that she did during the late 1920s, she has now moved on to oil painting.

> C: She never took formal lessons?
> S: No.

C: Would she teach you to do it or let you play …

S: I would be quite happy to just sit and watch her.[2]

Her paintings, in a somewhat naïve style, usually depict landscapes. But she also paints flowers with an innate sense of harmony and colour. She doesn't hesitate to display her paintings and delights in giving them as presents to her children and grandchildren.

Painting, "Canoe on a River" by Marie-Louise

Painting, "Village on Water's Edge" by Marie-Louise

She has other hobbies such as reading. But since she never had the occasion to learn formally to read and write, this pastime remains occasional. She does read children's books to her granddaughter, and leafs through magazines or *Reader's Digest*, but she much prefers television.

> She just loved *Ed Sullivan* and *Laugh In*. She enjoyed the comedy shows for sure[3]. … She had a TV in her room and she was a bit more of a night owl than the rest of us were, and so she had an earphone and she would look at the TV and she would laugh and laugh at TV shows she was watching. And so this is my memory of her, sitting and laughing by herself with the TV and just having a great time.[4]

Always Keeping the Secret

Marie-Louise ages gracefully. Her silver hair accentuates the softness of her comely face. Her grandson Jean-Pierre tells me that, at this period, her most striking trait was her eyes. *"It was her eyes, I remember, that were so warm. It was inviting."*[5]

But the long hours of work and the troubles she has known throughout her life take a toll on her heart. One day while visiting her son Joe, she has a heart attack. She is transported by ambulance to the Sacré-Coeur Hospital in Hull where she is admitted under the name Marie-Louise Ray.

One day when Gertrude is at her bedside, a nun enters the room and, after introducing herself, asks Marie-Louise, *"You wouldn't be Marie-Louise Bouchard by any chance?"*

To Gertrude's great astonishment, Marie-Louise denies her maiden name. When the sister leaves, Gertrude asks her mother why she refused to admit that she was Marie-Louise Bouchard. She answers, *"Leave it alone."*

To this day, Gertrude wonders who this nun was and how she had known her mother. Was she a native of Hanmer? Why did Marie-Louise insist on hiding her real name from her? Since she was registered under the name Marie-Louise Ray, we can surmise that she didn't want to engage in a conversation that would have led to speak of her "marriage" and of her "husband."

Once again, and in spite of all the years that have passed, her promise to Joseph to never speak of him to anyone has prevented her from establishing a relationship and has locked her up in an embarrassing silence.

REMINISCENCES OF LONG AGO

As she gets older, Marie-Louise finds herself thinking more and more about her childhood. Sometimes she feels the need to confide a little. So she talks about some distant memories surfacing in her mind: her life as a little girl in Hanmer, all the work she had to do in the house, and the trip her parents made from Les Escoumins to Hanmer.

> *My grandmother ... spoke of Les Escoumins. ... She spoke about the trip they had made when she was young ... when they left Les Escoumins. ... She spoke to me about that trip as if it had been a huge feat in those days. I guess her parents must have told her about it afterwards, you know. ... But it appeared to me that she did not remember what Les Escoumins really was.*[6]

But such disclosures are brief and infrequent, because Marie-Louise jealously guards the doors on her past.

THE BLOOMERS

Nanny appreciates more than ever the moments of relaxation she can spend with her grandchildren. She maintains a close relationship with them, which says a lot about her innate sensitivity since, generally speaking, the relationship between grandchildren and grandparents tends to fade with adolescence. Her undeniable sense of humour astounds them sometimes, especially when she laughs about the minor misadventures happening to her.

> *She loved to laugh; she loved to play cards, and to enjoy herself. I remember going to Mass with her one Sunday. We lived in Sandy Hill and we walked along Laurier Avenue to get to Sacré-Coeur Church. So, half-way there, her bloomers fell down around her ankles. The elastic broke and so they fell down. She just picked them up and put them in her purse. And we laughed. We went to church. And she thought it was very amusing to attend Mass with a bare bum!*[7]

At that time, women wore girdles to flatten their stomach. And fashion dictated that over the girdle one would wear fairly wide underpants called bloomers to hide the girdle and preserve the feminine modesty. As Nanny sews her underwear, one might expect that after this minor adventure she would sew in elastic strong enough to hold back a rabid dog. But the girdle material is very slippery ...

> *Mom asked me to go to the IGA with Nanny. As we were going down an aisle —and it was the middle of winter— her red flannelette bloomers fell down at her ankles. I was so embarrassed that I continued to walk pretending that I didn't know her.*
> [She laughs.]

After that, she caught up with me but she had just picked them up and put them in her bag.[8]

THE BRAID

Nanny finds ways to weave very personal ties with her grandchildren by making from time to time a discreet gesture that touches their heart.

> **L:** *When I was about 18 or 20, she gave me her hair.*
> *... I think I was going to a ball. ... And she brought*
> *it in and said, "If you wish to wear it." She had*
> *kept a beautiful braid that I wore for a few years.*
> *If I had a ball or a special occasion, the hairdresser*
> *would put it on me and would fix it. And I was so*
> *proud to wear my grandmother's hair.*
> **C:** *Was the hair auburn or very red?*
> **L:** *Auburn, but quite copper. A true auburn. And*
> *very thick, you know.*[9]

THIEVES

Not surprising that everyone in the family loves her. Everyone feel somewhat protective about her as she ages, and when a misfortune befalls her, they all take to the barricades.

Nanny is in the habit of taking the bus to get to Gertrude's. One day as she walks toward the house after her bus ride, thieves attack her and steal her purse. I ask Gertrude how her mother had reacted:

> **C:** *She must have had a shock! And you must have*
> *had one, too.*

G: *Yes, yes. But in those days things like that didn't*
   happen very often. It was rather rare.
C: *Did she recover quickly?*
G: *Oh yes, in fact I found that she was very tough.*
C: *She was not letting things get her down.*
G: *Oh no. Because when you think about everything*
   she went through and that she was not discouraged.
   Really you know. I think I would have died, for sure.[10]
[We laugh together.]

The news dismays the whole family.

> She was all black and blue! ... Everybody was so
> upset![11]

How could anyone dare assault their Nanny? She is almost 78 years
old. Who is coward enough to attack a woman of that age? Thankfully, she is not seriously wounded.

As for the purse, it surfaces the following spring under a melt-
ing snow bank, like a bad memory surfacing in the mind. It is
empty.

CHAPTER TEN

1970 TO *1973*

Living in Peace

> For everything there is a season, and a
> time for every matter under heaven:
> ... a time to weep, and a time to laugh
> ... a time to be born, and a time to die
>
> ✐ ECCLESIASTES 3

Housewarming

In 1970, Nanny has a big surprise in store for the family. Like a young student who leaves home to live in her own apartment, Nanny at age 79 moves out of Lorne's home and rents an apartment in a seniors' residence on Rochester Street in front of the High School of Commerce.

The family helps her to settle. She doesn't have very much to move. The successive moves over the course of her lifetime have reduced her possessions to her bedroom furniture. Gertrude provides her with household articles and Nanny soon gives her apartment a very personal character. When I ask her granddaughter to describe the apartment to me, she tells me:

> A nice little apartment, neat and tidy with paintings, usually something up on the easel and a few plants. A neat, little apartment.[1]

Marie-Louise finally has her own place and everybody observes the tremendous joy that she feels.

> *I think it's the first time that I saw her truly happy.*[2]

> I still recognize just the joy that she felt in finally being on her own, just as if she finally reached the goal that she always wanted to do, not to be dependent on somebody else at some point. She wasn't there for very long ... but she LOVED that time.[3]

But on 28 December of that same year, a cloud comes to shade her happiness. Her sister Claire-Hilda passes away in Hanmer. Marie-Louise goes to Hanmer with Gertrude and her husband to attend the funeral. She says goodbye to her "twin gossip," her confidant, the little sister that she had seen born with so much joy and that she couldn't have imagined dying before her.

Upon her return from Hanmer, Marie-Louise's social life becomes organized around a new circle of friends and she spends even more time on her creative activities.

> *She started going to the movies with her girlfriends in the building, and taking painting lessons, then pottery classes and really, you know, it was a blossoming, it was the youth she never had.*[4]

Her relationship with her family takes another turn. It is she, now, who receives them.

> *I remember that she welcomed me in her apartment. She was so proud to show me all her things.*[5]

Her grandchildren visit her regularly and if, per chance, other building residents take the elevator at the same time, Marie-Louise does not deprive herself of the pleasure to proudly introduce them.

> She would be so happy if somebody came in the elevator 'cause it would be somebody else she could introduce me to. And she had quite a few grandchildren and I am sure they all got the same treatment if they would go and visit. Oh yeah, she was very happy to show off her grandchildren.[6]

Members of the family surround her with great care as she always did for them. On Sunday nights, Lorne comes to pick her up, takes her to his home for dinner and brings her back at the end of the evening. Her granddaughters help with her household chores and Marie-Louise, as always, expresses her gratitude with little treats much appreciated.

*I remember her apartment because I had gone to wash
her floors and she had given me a box of chocolates.
My God, that impressed me! A whole box of chocolates
just for me!* Oh wow![7]

Wedding of Michael Ray, grandson of Marie-Louise, 21 July 1973.
Nanny is to the left of the groom.

ARTIST

Marie-Louise continues to partake in activities organized by the
Good Companions' Club that she had joined a few years earlier.
But the activity she always prefers and that she comes back to time
and again is, without doubt, painting in oils. She has installed her
easel in her living room and paints, alone and inspired, in the peace
of her apartment.

> She had taken up painting and gave my parents a
> painting she made, that, at the time, I felt was spec-
> tacular. She was very proud of it, and was happy
> that we were impressed with her work.[8]

Some of her paintings still adorn the houses of her children and grandchildren. They are signed "L. Ray."

Painting, flower pot

A TIME TO DIE

In the summer of 1973, Marie-Louise learns that one of her granddaughters, Louise Mantha, is moving to Japan for a few years with her husband. In mid August, at the moment of departure, Nanny's reaction takes her breath away.

The whole family came to the airport to say goodbye.
And when I arrived at my grandmother, I kissed her
and she said, "I will never see you again." And I said,
"For heaven's sake, Nanny, why do you say that?" [9]

They say that when death is near, we get premonitory signals: a dream, thoughts linked to death, the desire to express feelings kept silent until then or an urgent need to settle legal affairs. Perhaps this separation from a granddaughter that she loves tenderly and the great distance that will prevent them from visiting from time to time awakens in Marie-Louise a portent of her imminent death. Installed in Japan, Louise starts corresponding with her grandmother. Nanny attempts to answer her in spite of her limited abilities in written communication. Louise notes with tender astonishment that her Nanny is simply illiterate.

She was illiterate! The letters she wrote to me were all
phonetic. She didn't know how to spell. [10]

In the month of October following Louise's departure, Marie-Louise learns that she must go to hospital for an operation. At the moment of leaving for the hospital, she feels anxious.

Mum and I went to pick her up at her apartment to bring her to the hospital. When we got there she said, "Christina, if I don't come home, you can have my TV" … And mum kept saying, "No, no. You will be back on Monday. Don't worry about it." She said, "Just in case, this plant needs this and don't forget my poinsettia," and this and that and she kept insisting — and THAT I will never forget because she would never get compulsive. Somehow she knew. [11]

During the operation, she has a heart attack. When notified of the situation, the family rushes to her bedside.

> **D:** Dad [Joe] and Gertrude for sure stayed with
> Nanny in hospital. … Her heart was failing.
> So they went and spent the night with her.
> And she died and then Dad came over to my
> house to tell me that she had died.
> **C:** And I am sure he was terribly affected.
> **D:** He was! He was! I did not expect that. I didn't
> expect her to die. She was going in for a D & C.[12]
> … She had congestive heart failure. … So her
> heart couldn't take the anaesthetic.[13]

Now that Nanny is deceased, Diane is pleased that she had a last chance to spoil her a little before her departure for the hospital.

> I remember that I was very happy that I had brought
> her that beautiful plant because she was going in to
> be operated on and I thought, "Why wait till she is
> in the hospital? I will give it to her now." And I am so
> glad I did because she died! … I was so happy because
> she was so thrilled with that and I was remembering
> that present you know [she is referring to the incident
> with the perfume bottle]. I was trying to make up for
> so many years. But that did it because it was for no
> reason. And I just drop by, out of the blue, brought
> her this beautiful Chrysanthemum. She was very,
> very touched, excited. I felt really good.[14]

On 23 October 1973 at the age of 82, Marie-Louise Labelle née Bouchard passes away. In Notre Dame Cemetery on Montreal Road, her tombstone reads:

RAY
Marie L. Bouchard
Wife of Joseph Ray
1891–1973

Engraved in the stone, in capital letters, is the name Ray, the alias that she and Joseph adopted to hide their love. And in spite of the fact that Joseph never officially married her, the inscription attests to her full right to the title of wife: "Wife of Joseph Ray." No mention is made of her adoptive name, Labelle. She returns to the earth with her maiden name of Bouchard. She has come full circle.

One day when Gertrude and her daughter Suzanne visit Marie-Louise's grave, Gertrude whispers, *"She lied all the way to her grave!"* [15]

Grave of Marie-Louise Bouchard Labelle

Epilogue

On 12 July 2005, Albert Laurent Ray (Lorne) died in Ottawa, leaving Gertrude as the sole survivor of Marie-Louise's three children.

At the moment of concluding this book, in August 2007, Marie-Louise Bouchard Labelle and Joseph Ray (Jérémie Alphonse Roy) had 13 grandchildren and 22 great grandchildren. The unconditional love and unfailing devotion that Marie-Louise brought to raising her children after their father's departure have left an indelible mark on this large family where humour combines with love, generosity, frankness and self-giving.

In early January 2008, destiny helped me bring closure to this story that kept haunting me and of which I was hoping so much to uncover the last secrets. The publisher to whom I had submitted my manuscript sent it to an independent evaluator. One of the comments made by this evaluator suggested a research avenue unknown to me until then. It was with a pounding heart that, in searching through the tomes of this new source of information, I found out what became of Father Roy after he left his family in 1928.

The Church first sent him to the Saint Antoine Hospice in the village of St-Lin (now St-Lin-Laurentides) 30 kilometres north of Montreal in the present Lanaudière administrative region, at the foot of the Laurentians. This institution was run by the Sisters of Providence from Montreal. Then in 1933, at 75 years of age, he was transferred to the Saint Janvier Residence at 795 Gouin Boulevard in north Montreal. The following year, this Residence moved to 1801 Gouin Boulevard East. In 1935, Father Roy replaced Mr. Alfred L'Ecuyer as Chaplin at the Residence, a position that he occupied until 1943. During this period, the Residence opened a crèche, the Saint Paul Crèche, administered by the Sisters of Mercy. In 1943, Father Jean-Louis Chartrand became the Residence's new Chaplin. Father Roy, who was then 85 years old, stayed at the Saint Janvier Residence, and this is where he died on 28 July 1944, without saying goodbye to Marie-Louise and the children.

Gertrude in front the grave of her father's, J.A. Roy

Postscript

THE CATHOLIC CHURCH, WOMEN, AND PRIESTS' CELIBACY

This book was written because the time had come to talk about Marie-Louise's story before the last witnesses to her life pass away. The research I conducted has convinced me that it is also time to talk openly about the relationship between the Catholic Church and women.

The Catholic Church does not recognize equality of the sexes. It justifies its position by quoting the Bible where, in Genesis, a woman is made from a man's rib and tempts him with an apple. The mythical image of this woman as both stemming from man and being his temptress is still well anchored in the psyche of the Catholic Church's representatives. This mental programming is the basis upon which woman's status has been defined in the Christian world for a long period of our history.

In the early twentieth century, the Church conferred on women a limited and strictly defined role: the Church praised the woman servant. It bestowed on her the title of "Servant of God" when she took the veil and that of "Queen of the household" when she carried out her role of wife and mother in service of her husband and children. As well, the Church commended women who devoted themselves to serving the sick, the career of nursing having the status of a vocation. Apart from these well-defined limits, women had very little credit in the Church's eyes. They remained a subordinate whose judgment was easily and frequently called into question.

In this beginning of the twenty-first century, the image of woman as a temptress leading man into sin persists in the Catholic Church. When a Catholic priest and a woman have a liaison as consenting adults, it is the woman who, in the eyes of the Church, is generally perceived as the instigator. And so when it comes time to find solutions to the problems generated by such a liaison, the woman's happiness and that of her children carry very little weight in the Church's decision making. Recently, some women have decided to disclose this situation by publishing their love story with a Catholic priest. Their actions publicly open the debate concerning the relationship between the Catholic Church and women.

I hope that this biography of Marie-Louise Bouchard Labelle provides these pioneers with a historical perspective on the question of the mandatory celibacy of Catholic priests by demonstrating how this practice already had terrible consequences in the early twentieth century. What difference has a century brought to this practice and to the way in which we manage its consequences?

Appendices

Appendix One

Arrival in Hanmer

During Hanmer's 25th anniversary, an article in the *Sudbury Star* from 20 June 1923, recounts this memorable event:

> An event unique in the history of the district will be celebrated at Hanmer this week in the anniversary of the coming of the first settlers. ... Twenty-five years ago, Jacob Proulx, Henry Beaulieu, Napoléon Labelle and Joseph Chartrand came to the district and settled at what is now known as Hanmer. On April 20th, 1898, they arrived in the district. With the exception of Mr. Chartrand, they were married men, with families. Jacob Proulx, 51 years of age when he settled in Hanmer, had a family of nine; Henri Beaulieu, 41 years of age, had a family of seven, and Napoléon Labelle, 33 years of age, had a family of four. (See note 1 below.)

The journalist rounds up a bit the truth. First of all, Napoléon is not quite 33 years old. Since he was born on 24 October 1866, he is only 32 years old. As for his family of four, it is really more like a family of three and a half: Napoléon, Georgianne, Marie-Louise and a baby to be born.

Mrs. Huguette Parent, in her document *The Township of Hanmer* 1904–1969 went back to the Sudbury Star article and translated it into French. Her translation states that Napoléon is 33 years old and has 4 children. If this is true, it would mean that between May 1895, the date of her second marriage, and 1898, Georgianne would have given birth to 3 children: Claire-Hilda, Paul and Dorilla. It is possible because we know that at that time, births were numerous and close together. But according to the information that I found, Claire-Hilda, the oldest of the three, was born in Copper Cliff on 15 October 1898; Paul was born in Hanmer on 8 October 1900; and his baby sister Dorilla was also born in Hanmer in 1903. Therefore, Napoléon had only two children — Marie-Louise and the baby to come — when they moved to Hanmer in April 1898.

So why does Mrs. Parent write that he had four children? One has to consult the original article in English to find the answer. It reads "… and Napoléon Labelle, 33 years of age, had a family of four." A family of four: Napoléon, Georgianne, Marie-Louise and Claire-Hilda (yet unborn). The sentence in English could effectively be misconstrued and lead Mrs. Parent to write, "N. Labelle, 33 years, has four (children)." (See note 2 below.)

Notes:

1. Reprint of the story which appeared in the Sudbury Star on 20 June 1923. Greater Sudbury Library.

2. Parent, Huguette, Le Township de Hanmer 1904–1969. Historical documents #70. The Historical Society of New Ontario, University of Sudbury 1979, p. 12.

Appendix Two

HOUSE IN HANMER

It is hard to believe that Napoléon and Georgianne would have lived in a three-sided house. It is probable that Napoléon and his three companions lived in such a dwelling while they were clearing their lots. But given the fact that Georgianne arrives in the dead of winter (December 1898) with a 7-year-old child and a 2-month-old baby, it is logical to expect that Napoléon had built a regular round-log house. Indeed, if we use as a testimonial the photo of a house built the same year by Mr. Jacob Proulx, one of Napoléon's pioneer companions, we can maintain that the house built by Napoléon was a round-log house since all the houses in this era were built the same way.

Napoléon must certainly have built the furniture, too. A gifted craftsman, all his life he took intense pleasure from working with wood. His granddaughters still have in their possession some very nice chairs built by their grandfather.

Appendix Three

LANDOWNER

An analysis of landownership in the municipalities of Hanmer and Capreol conducted by Laurentian University (see note 1 below) reveals that in 1912, Father J.A. Roy owns no less than seven lots or parts of lots in these districts. (See the map of the landowners in part of the Districts of Hanmer and Capreol in December 1912 appearing on page 526 of Guy Gaudreau's document listed below.)

I verified the ownership at the Land Title Office of Sudbury. Two of the lots shown on the map as belonging to him are not registered in his name. They were given to the Church by parishioners in 1907 and 1909, probably to build the church and the presbytery. Four other lots are definitely registered in his name. I could not find any information about the seventh one. However, in addition to the lots mentioned by Mr. Gaudreau, he would also have been the first owner of part of lot 9, Concession VI in the County of Blezard, according to the County map published in *Valley East 1850–2002*. (See note 2 below.)

That a Catholic priest would own land does raise questions as confirmed by the analyst's comments:

> *One case deserves attention, although it is not a farmer's case. It concerns Joseph Alphonse Roy, first curate of the parish Saint Jacques in Hanmer. One could be astonished at the extent of his property holdings.*

However, everything happens as though it would be a
strategy to preserve the homogeneity — religious and
possibly cultural — of his parish. At least, that is the
hypothesis that we would like to advance. The priest
buys back lands from departing parishioners probably
in order to sell them to new parishioners in due course,
new parishioners that he no doubt selects himself. The
curate would therefore play a far more active role in
colonization than we would have believed. (See note
3 below.)

What to think about such a hypothesis? The Church's methods
to ensure a French-Catholic presence across Canada, mentioned
in Chapter 2, would justify perfectly this hypothesis. But we have
no proof. The results of my research do indicate that Father Roy
sold most of his property to French pioneers but did he do it to
exercise a friendly and discreet control on the choice of parishioners or simply because the purchaser just happened to be French
and Catholic? Since he was aware of the Church's colonization
objectives, I think he was conscious of the importance of giving
first choice to a French-Catholic pioneer but he certainly did not
feel overly obligated by the Church's mission since in 1925 he sells
one of his lots in the township of Hanmer to an anglophone.

What really arouses one's curiosity about a priest buying so
much real estate is the financial question. Where did Father Roy
get the money to buy all these lots? Actually, the secular clergy
does not make a vow of poverty and the curate of a parish receives
from the Church a modest salary for his services. But is it enough
to buy all this land? Perhaps he had saved money in the preceding
years? Who knows?

One thing is certain. These purchases mean that he is not merely
the curate in the village. He has become a property owner and a
property owner with a certain social power because generally, a

pioneer in Hanmer or Capreol would own only one or two lots. However, he owns five of them! Thus, he would have his say when comes time to discuss issues concerning the township's development.

Notes:

1. Gaudreau, Guy *Les activités forestières dans deux communautés agricoles du Nouvel-Ontario, 1900–1920*. In Revue historique de l'Amérique française, pp. 501–529.

2. Lebelle, Wayne F., *Valley East* 1850–2002, p. 82.

3. Gaudreau, *Les activités forestières*, p. 527.

Appendix Four

Amour Immaculé

Je sais en une église un vitrail merveilleux
Où quelque artiste illustre, inspiré des archanges,
A peint d'une façon mystique, en robe à franges,
Le front nimbé d'un astre, une Sainte aux yeux bleus.

Le soir, l'esprit hanté de rêves nébuleux
Et du céleste écho de récitals étranges,
Je m'en viens la prier sous les lueurs oranges
De la lune qui luit entre ses blonds cheveux.

Telle, sur le vitrail de mon cœur je t'ai peinte,
Ma romanesque aimée, ô pâle et blonde sainte,
Toi, la seule que j'aime et toujours j'aimerai,

Toi qui restes muette, impassible et qui, fière,
Peut-être me verras, sombre et désespéré,
Errer dans mon amour comme en un cimetière!

Poème d'Émile Nelligan tiré de L'École littéraire de Montréal, *Les soirées du Château de Ramezay*, Montréal, Eusèbe Senécal & Cie, 1900, p. 313.

IMMACULATE LOVE

I know a marvellous stained glass window in a church
Where some illustrious artist, inspired by the archangels,
Painted in a mystical fashion, in a fringed robe,
The forehead crowned with a star, a Saint with blue eyes.

In the evening, the mind haunted by nebulous dreams
And by the celestial echo of strange recitals,
I come to pray her under the orange glow
Of the moon that shines on her blond hair.

As on the stained glass of my heart, I painted you,
My romantic beloved, O pale and fair saint,
You, the only one I love and will always love,

You, who stay silent, impassive and proud,
Perhaps you will see me, sombre and desperate,
Wander in my love as in a cemetery!

Poem by Émile Nelligan, from *The Literary School of Montreal: Evenings at Chateau Ramezay* (Montreal, Quebec: Eusèbe Senécal & Co, 1900), p. 313.

Translation by Claire Trépanier and Renata Brunner Jass. No translation of this poem was found in translated, collected works of Nelligan.

Certificate of Birth of Désiré Jérémie Roy

du régistre des baptêmes, mariages et sépultures de la paroisse de

AINT-MARCELLIN DE LES ESCOUMINS, CTÉ SAGUENAY, P. Q., CANADA
DIOCÈSE DU GOLFE-ST-LAURENT

e mil huit cent quatre-vingt onze.

Le premier octobre mil huit cent quatre-vingt onze, nous prêtre missionnaire soussigné avons baptisé Marie-Louise, née la veille fille légitime de Théophile Bouchard, journalier, et de Georgianne Tremblay des Escoumins. La parrain a été Jean Bouchard, oncle de l'enfant, et la marraine Catherine Dion, sa femme qui ont signé avec nous, le père absent.
Lecture faite.

Jean Bouchard
Catherine Dion

C. L Parent, ptre., V.F.

Certificate of Birth of Marie-Louise Bouchard

Dated   August 16th,   1930

JOSEPH ROY

TO

MARIE LOUISE RAY

Deed of Land

SITUATE

Lots 133,134,135,187,188,189
Rideau Park.   Plan 129

DYE & DURHAM. 9-11 YONGE-STREET ARCADE. TORONTO. CAN.

Without search or investigation
of title.

RETURN TO   RAOUL MERCIER,
             Barrister,Solicitor
             45 Rideau Street,
             Ottawa, Ontario,

Notarized document dated 16 August 1930,
showing the transfer of land titles from Joseph **Roy** to Marie-Louise **Ray**, p. 1

This Indenture

made (in Duplicate) the   sixteenth   day of August
one thousand nine hundred and thirty

In Pursuance of The Short Forms of Conveyances Act:

Between

JOSEPH ROY of the Township of Gloucester
in the County of Carleton in the Province
of Ontario, Yeoman, hereinafter the GRANTOR

OF THE FIRST PART

A N D :

MARIE LOUISE RAY, of the same place,
Widow, hereinafter the GRANTEE

OF THE SECOND PART

Witnesseth that in consideration of Fifteen hundred - - - - - - - - -

- - - - - -($1500.00)- - - - - - - - - - - - - - - - **Dollars**
of lawful money of Canada now paid by the said Grantee   to the said
Grantor   (the receipt whereof is hereby by him   acknowledged),

Notarized document dated 16 August 1930 showing the transfer of land titles
from Joseph **Roy** to Marie-Louise **Ray, widow,** for the sum of $1,500, p. 2

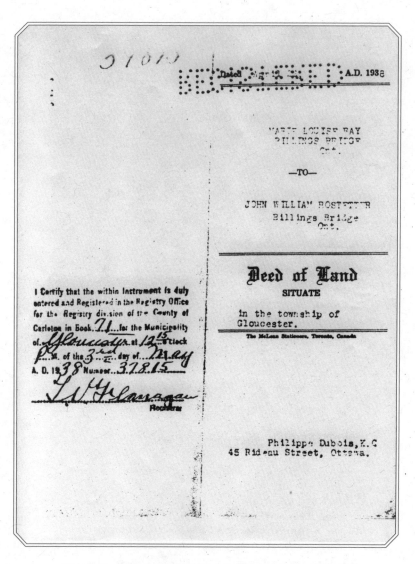

Deed of sale for the Rideau Park lots by Marie-Louise Ray
to John William Rostetter, 3 May 1938

Death Certificate of D. Jérémie A. Roy, who died on 28 July 1944

Note written by Marie-Louise indicating her children's
birthdates and birthplaces

To wish you the blessings
of a Joyous Christmas and a Happy New Year

Dear Ken Diane hope to see you
soon hope youve all in good health
we all in good health . . . hope you be
comming to Hoorie miding
I often think of you Load of Love

Christmas card written by Marie-Louise to her granddaughter Diane Ray

LIST OF PEOPLE INTERVIEWED

(In the order in which they were interviewed)

1. Gertrude Mantha, born Gertrude Ray, second child of Marie-Louise Bouchard Labelle and J.A. Roy.

2. Louise Mantha, Gertrude's daughter and granddaughter of Marie-Louise Bouchard Labelle and J.A. Roy.

3. Suzanne Mantha, Gertrude's daughter and granddaughter of Marie-Louise Bouchard Labelle and J.A. Roy.

4. Albert Laurent "Lorne" Ray, third child of Marie-Louise Bouchard Labelle and J.A. Roy.

5. Valery Ray née Bennett, second wife of Albert Laurent "Lorne" Ray.

6. David Ray, Lorne's son and grandson of Marie-Louise Bouchard Labelle and J.A. Roy, in Calgary, Alberta.

7. Clothilde Bergeron Baelde, niece of Marie-Louise, in Hanmer, Ontario.

8. Georgette Bergeron, niece of Marie-Louise, in Hanmer, Ontario.

9. DesNeiges Bergeron, niece of Marie-Louise, in Hanmer, Ontario.

10. Cathy Ray Steele, Lorne's daughter and granddaughter of Marie-Louise, in Manotick, Ontario.

11. Anne Mantha Letellier, Gertrude's daughter and granddaughter of Marie-Louise Bouchard Labelle and J.A. Roy.

12. Albert Mantha, Gertrude's son and grandson of Marie-Louise Bouchard Labelle and J.A. Roy. (via letter)

13. Patrick Mantha, Gertrude's son and grandson of Marie-Louise Bouchard Labelle and J.A. Roy.

14. Pauline Mantha, Gertrude's daughter and granddaughter of Marie-Louise Bouchard Labelle and J.A. Roy.

15. Jean-Pierre Mantha, Gertrude's son and grandson of Marie-Louise Bouchard Labelle and J.A. Roy.

16. Diane Ray Parker, Joe's daughter and granddaughter of Marie-Louise Bouchard Labelle and J.A. Roy.

17. Donald Ray, Joe's son and grandson of Marie-Louise Bouchard Labelle and J.A. Roy. (via e-mail)

18. Michael Ray, Joe's son and grandson of Marie-Louise Bouchard Labelle and J.A. Roy.

19. Christina Ray Richardson, Joe's daughter and granddaughter of Marie-Louise Bouchard Labelle and J.A. Roy.

20. Frank Mansfield, who lived through the Great Depression in Ottawa and who willingly, shared his memories. A very grateful posthumous thank you.

21. Oliver Wendell Williams, a friend of Frank Mansfield, who also lived through the Great Depression in Ottawa and who participated in the interview with Frank.

22. Daniel J. Kealey, ex-Catholic priest, President of the company People in Development. He briefed me on the hierarchy and rules in the Catholic Church.

List of People Who Helped Me in My Research

Thanks to all of you who guided me in my research. Some of you I never even met in person. It is one of the negative aspects of modern technology that, although it permits us to easily communicate at a distance, deprives us at the same time of the great pleasure of shaking hands with the person with whom we are communicating. Perhaps one day I will have the pleasure of meeting you in person.

1. Lynn Keating, nurse in Wolseley, Saskatchewan whose assistance have been particularly precious to me. She found the photo of Father Roy and gave me the name of a priest on assignment in Rome. All my friendship!

2. Sister Ria Gerritsen, SCSL, archivist in Archdiocese of Regina, Saskatchewan. She found handwritten letters from Father Roy and allowed me to photocopy them. Thank you for this priceless source of information.

3. Sister Leona, with the Diocese of Medicine Hat, Alberta. (via e-mail)

4. Father Donald Bolen, priest from Saskatchewan on temporary assignment in Rome. (via e-mail)

5. Dr. Luca Carboni, Vatican Archivist. (via letter)

6. Susan Fortin, a perfect stranger I met at the Land Registry Office of the city of Ottawa. She was kind enough to help me find legal documents on microfiche and to interpret them for me. She was there doing research for a friend and ended up helping me with part of mine.

7. André Lalonde, historian, University of Regina, Saskatchewan. (via telephone)

8. Laurier Gareau, ex-President of the Saskatchewan Historical Society. (via telephone)

9. Tim Novak, Archivist, Saskatchewan Archives Board, Regina, Saskatchewan. (via e-mail)

10. Dave Yanko, Virtual Saskatchewan. (via e-mail)

11. Rev. Anthony Man Son-Hing, Chancellor Secretary to the Bishop, Diocese of Sault Ste Marie, Sudbury Ontario. (via e-mail)

12. Nina Prestera, who translated into Italian my letters to the Vatican Archivist.

13. Diana Frey, St. Patrick Catholic Church, Medicine Hat, Alberta. She found a contact for me in the Medicine Hat Diocese. (via e-mail)

14. Monsignor Angelo Caruso, Diocese of Sault Ste Marie, Sudbury, Ontario. (via e-mail)

15. Marie-Louise Perron, Canadian Centre for Genealogy, Division of References and Genealogy, Library and Archives Canada, Ottawa.

16. Michelle Landriault, Land Title Office, Sudbury, Ontario.

17. Jim Fortin, Curator, City of Greater Sudbury Heritage Museum. (via e-mail)

18. Clara Fouillard, Chancery Archives, Kamloops, B.C. (via e-mail)

19. Nada Mehes-Rovinelli, Archivist, Greater Sudbury Public Library. Mrs. Mehes-Rovinelli was of great assistance to me. She patiently guided me through the archives and microfilms in the library and shared with me her extensive knowledge on the history of mining in New Ontario.

20. Serge Barbe, Archivist, City of Ottawa Archives. (via e-mail)

21. Harriette Fried, Reference assistant, City of Ottawa Archives. (via e-mail)

22. Juliette Champagne, Edmonton. The reference she suggested that I consult led me to find the data on Father Roy's last years.

Abbreviated Chronology

(AS OF AUGUST 2007)

30 October 1858: Birth of Désiré Jérémie Roy in Bethierville, Quebec.

28 February 1888: J.A. Roy is ordained a priest by Mgr Fabre.

1890–1905: J.A. Roy is a missionary in the Canadian West.

30 September 1891: Birth of Marie-Louise Bouchard in Les Escoumins. Quebec.

1 October 1891: Baptism of Marie-Louise Bouchard in St. Marcellin parish in Les Escoumins.

1893: Death of Marie-Louise's father, Théophile Bouchard, in a mining accident in Copper Cliff

13 May 1895: Marie-Louise's mother, Georgianne Tremblay, weds Napoléon Labelle.

December 1898: The family moves to Hanmer, Ontario (slightly north of Sudbury).

1 August 1906: J.A. Roy becomes the first curate in Hanmer.

29 September 1913: End of J.A. Roy's term as curate in Hanmer.

1913–1916: Father Roy is the curate in Cache Bay.

1916: Marie-Louise and Joseph flee Cache Bay and come to live in Ottawa.

12 April 1917: Birth of Joseph Ray, first child of Marie-Louise Bouchard Labelle and J.A. Roy (who now uses the name Joseph Ray).

21 May 1917: Joseph Ray (alias J.A. Roy) buys from William Slinn Lots 133, 134 and 135 on Stanley Avenue as well as Lots 187, 188 and 189 facing on Billings Avenue in Rideau Park.

1917–1928: Joseph Ray (alias Jérémie Alphonse Roy) lives on Stanley Avenue with Marie-Louise and their children.

30 October 1918: Birth of Gertrude Ray, second child of Marie-Louise Bouchard Labelle and Joseph Ray (alias Jérémie Alphonse Roy). Joseph is 60 years old!

1 November 1920: Death of Georgianne Tremblay, Marie-Louise's mother, in Hanmer. Marie-Louise attends her mother's funeral with her son Joe. She is pregnant with her son Lorne.

16 March 1921: Birth of Albert Laurent Ray (known as Lorne), third child of Marie-Louise and Joseph Ray (alias Jérémie Alphonse Roy).

28 March 1928: Mgr. Forbes becomes Archbishop of Ottawa.

1928: Jérémie Alphonse Roy (alias Joseph Ray) returns to the priesthood.

Thursday, 24 October 1929: The New-York Stock Exchange crashes. Beginning of the Great Depression.

16 August 1930: Joseph Roy (alias Joseph Ray) transfers 6 lots to Marie-Louise. The notarized document states that Joseph *Roy* transfers the property titles to Marie-Louise *Ray, widow.*

1930–1932: Marie-Louise rents the house to Mr. Baker and family. She and the children move to the second floor of a house located on Bank St, between Cameron and Riverdale. She runs the lunch counter attached to the house but the business fails.

1932: Marie-Louise and the children move to the second floor of a house at 402 Sunnyside.

Spring 1933: Marie-Louise and the children move back to the house on Stanley Avenue. The Bakers continue to occupy the house until the fall.

1933–1935: The Great Depression worsens. Trips to Montreal. Marie-Louise and a friend rent a house on Second Ave in the Glebe and transform it into a convalescent home. The project is a fiasco and they lose their investment. Marie-Louise has a small kiosk constructed by the side of the house to sell sodas and candy. New failure.

1935–1936: Penniless, Marie-Louise rents the Stanley Avenue house to John W. Rostetter and moves with the children to a three-bedroom home at 187 James St. One can surmise that Joseph A. Roy helped out because he sells one of his lots at a loss.

1936–1937: Marie-Louise rents an imposing three-story, eight-bedroom house on Lisgar St. and transforms it into a boarding house. Total bankruptcy! Her eldest son, Joe, goes to work in northern Ontario mines.

1937–1939: Marie-Louise moves to a three-story house at 227 Nepean. She sublets two rooms to bring in revenue.

3 May 1938: Marie-Louise finds herself gripped in a financial clutch and is forced to sell the Stanley Avenue house. She sells the lots to John Rostetter for $4,000. It is a sale with a big loss and she receives no cash since Mr. Rostetter has none either. He takes out a mortgage with her.

October 1938: Gertrude, Marie-Louise's daughter, leaves to study nursing in Cornwall.

July 1939: Marie-Louise and Lorne move to a small second floor apartment on Rideau St, at the corner of Chapel.

1 September 1939: Beginning of World War II.

1940: Marie-Louise gets a job cleaning federal government offices and moves with Lorne to a bachelor apartment on Slater St. (The house does not exist anymore.) Gertrude returns from Cornwall with tuberculosis and moves in with her mother and Lorne.

1941: Marie-Louise moves with Lorne and Gertrude to a three-story house at 5 Central Avenue. She rents out the top half of the house to a young couple.

1942: Gertrude returns to Cornwall to complete her Nursing Diploma.

3 December 1942: John Rostetter pays in full the balance of his mortgage with Marie-Louise. John Rostetter is now sole proprietor of the Stanley Avenue property.

1942–1943: DesNeiges Bergeron, Marie-Louise's niece from Hanmer, comes to work in Ottawa and lives with Marie-Louise on Central Avenue. Lorne is in the Navy and Gertrude is in Cornwall.

1 July 1943: Wedding of Joseph Ray (Marie-Louise's eldest son) with Marie Cécile Valois.

8 October 1943: Marriage of Lorne Ray (Marie-Louise's youngest son) with Isabella Hall.

Spring 1944: Gertrude completes her nursing degree and gets a job at the Ottawa General Hospital.

28 July 1944: Death of Jérémie Alphonse Roy in l'Assomption, QC.

31 July 1944: J.A. Roy is buried in Berthierville where he was born.

4 August 1944: Marie-Louise becomes a grandmother.

2 September 1945: End of the Second World War.

21 September 1946: Gertrude Ray (Marie-Louise's daughter) marries Paul-Émile Mantha.

1949: Marie-Louise is 58 years old. She leaves her government job and moves with Gertrude and her husband in Toronto where she will live until 1957.

1957: The Mantha family returns to Ottawa. Marie-Louise moves in with Lorne on Larose Avenue.

Spring 1960: Georgette Bergeron, Marie-Louise's godchild and niece, completes her nursing studies. Because Georgette's mother is in the hospital, Marie-Louise goes to Hanmer and stand in for her at the graduation ceremony.

1962–1965: The Mantha family has moved to 29 Sweetland Avenue. Marie-Louise still lives at Lorne's, but visits frequently and stays over from time to time.

September 1964: At 73 years of age, Marie-Louise travels to the Yukon with her sister Claire-Hilda, her sister's husband and her two nieces, Clothilde and Georgette Bergeron.

1970: Marie-Louise rents an apartment in a senior citizens residence on Rochester St. She devotes herself to oil painting.

28 December 1970: Claire-Hilda passes away. Marie-Louise attends her sister's funeral in Hanmer with her daughter Gertrude and her son-in-law Paul-Émile Mantha.

1973: Death of Marie-Louise Labelle (born Bouchard) in Ottawa. She is 82 years old. She is buried in Notre-Dame Cemetery in Ottawa, on Montreal Rd.

29 October 1994: In Aylmer, Quebec, death of Joseph Ray (Marie-Louise's eldest son)

12 July 2005: In Ottawa, death of Albert Laurent (Lorne) Ray (Marie-Louise's youngest son)

Notes

For interviews, page numbers noted are for unpublished transcripts in possession of the author.

Chapter 1

1   Gertrude Mantha, in a prepared recording, November 2004–March 2005.

2   Ibid.

3   Reference taken from and translated from the website "Histoire-Municipalité des Escoumins," pp. 2 & 3 (accessed March/April 2004).

4   Micheline Dumont et al. 1982. *L'histoire des femmes au Québec depuis quatre siècles* (Montréal, Quebec: Les Quinze), 140. Translated by Louise Mantha and Claire Trépanier.

5   *Sudbury Journal*, 2 November 1893: 1. Available in Bibliothèque publique de Sudbury.

6   Georgette Bergeron, interview with the author, 5 May 2005 (p. 15).

7   See Appendix 1: Arrival in Hanmer.

8   *Pionnières de chez nous*, recueil présénté par la [collection of stories presented by the] Fédération des femmes canadiennes-françaises de la Paroisse Saint-Jacques de Hanmer. Editions de l'Ami du people (Hanmer, p. 11).

9   Huguette Parent. Serie Pro-F-Ont., Centre franco-ontarien de ressources pédagogiques (Ottawa, 1980), pp. 35 & 36.

10 *Pionnières de chez nous*, p. 11).

11 Clothilde Bergeron, interview with the author, 4 May 2005 (p. 25).

12 See Appendix 2: House in Hanmer.

13 Dumont et al., *L'histoire des femmes au Québec*, p. 72.

14 Alfred Emery, *Bulletin paroissial de Paincourt*, 1914, told by Amédée Emery and quoted in *Villages et visages de l'Ontario français* by René Brodeur and Robert Choquette, Office de la télécommunication éducative de l'Ontario, 1979, p. 89.

15 Notes from the clerk-secretary taken at a municipal meeting in Hanmer and found in the school archives. I received a copy of these notes from Clothilde Bergeron.

16 *Pionnières de chez nous,* p. 12.

17 Miss Hotte no longer lives with the Labelles when Dorilla is born. She had married Léandre Frappier. But since the Labelles kept strong ties with her, they ask her to be Dorilla's godmother. Mr. and Mrs. Frappier thus both attend the christening as Dorilla's godmother and godfather.

18 Gertrude Mantha, interview with the author, 1 April 2004 (p. 12).

19 Clothilde Bergeron, interview with with author, 4 May 2005 (p. 1).

20 Georgette Bergeron, interview with the author, 5 May 2005 (pp. 27 & 29).

21 Wayne F. Labelle, *Valley East* 1850–2002 (WFL Communications), p. 151.

22 Gertude Mantha, interview with the author, 28 February 2006 (pp. 7 & 8).

23 *Farmers and Business Directory for the counties of Haliburton, Peterboro and Victoria and the districts of Muskoka, Parry Sound, Nipissing, Manitoulin, Rainy River, Thunder Bay and Keewatin.* 1906–7, Vol. XIV (Union Publishing Company of Ingersoll, 1906), p. 536.

Chapter 2

1 The 1908 edition of the *Dictionnaire biographique du clergé canadien-français* says it was on 26 February, 1888. The 1928 edition says it was on 28 February, 1888. I believe that the 1908 edition is correct, as it is corroborated by *Le Canada ecclésiastique.*

2 *The Encyclopaedia of Saskatchewan*, p. 450, quoted in http://sasksettlement. com.

3 Abbot Roméo Bédard, *History, Montmartre, Saskatchewan*, 1893–1953, Regina Dioscese, p. 16.

4 Letter from Albert Martelle to Archbishop Langevin dated 1 July 1895, Regina Archdiocese.

5 André lalonde, *Les canadiens français de l'Ouest; espoirs, tragédies, incertitudes,* on the internet site http://www.cefan.ulaval.ca/franco/my_html/LA-LONDE.html.

6 Bédard, *History, Montmartre, Sask.,* p. 24.

7 Bédard, *History, Montmartre, Sask.,* pp. 6 & 7.

8 Letter to Monsignor Langevin on 4 May 1901 from Father Passaplan, who replaced Father Roy in Wolseley.

9 Letter to Monsignor Langevin on 2 May 1900, Regina Archdiocese Archives.

10 Clothilde Bergeron, interview with the author, 4 May 2005 (p. 14).

11 On 19 August 1907, the Catholic Church buys for one dollar Lot 12 of Concession 11 of Capreol. It is probably on this site that Father Roy builds Hanmer's first chapel.

Chapter 3

1 See the Appendix 3: Landowner.

2 Georgette Bergeron, interview with the author, 5 May 2005 (p. 12).

3 Elizabeth Abbott, *Une histoire de maîtresses* (Editons Fides, 2004), p. 198.

4 Dumont et al., *L'histoire des femmes au Québec,* p. 279–280.

5 Gertrude Mantha, interview with the author, 1 April 2004 (p. 5).

6 Dumont et al., *L'histoire des femmes au Québec,* p. 172.

7 Dumont et al., *L'histoire des femmes au Québec,* p. 173.

8 Clothilde Bergeron, interview with the author, 4 May 2005 (p. 19).

9 Georgette Bergeron, interview with the author, 5 May 2005 (p. 14).

10 Gertrude Mantha, interview with the author, 29 November 2005 (p. 6).

Chapter 4

1 John Leaning, *The Story of the Glebe,* from the author (1999), p. 22.

2 John H. Taylor, *Ottawa, An Illustrated History* (Canadian Museum of Civilization, 1986), p. 120.

3   This house still exists although it has undergone renovations over the years. The current address is 279 Pleasant Park, the new name for Stanley Avenue.

4   Gerturde Mantha, in a prepared recording, November 2004–March 2005.

5   Gertrude Mantha, interview with the author, 1 April 2004 (p. 6).

6   Gertrude Mantha, interview with the author, 7 September 2004 (p. 17).

7   Gertrude Mantha, interview with the author, 1 April 2004 (p. 11).

8   Gertrude Mantha, interview with the author, 7 September 2004 (p. 17).

9   Gertrude Mantha, interview with the author, 1 April 2004 (p. 4).

10 Gertrude Mantha, interview with the author, 29 November 2005 (p. 16).

11 Gertrude Mantha, interview with the author, 10 August 2006 (pp. 7 & 8).

12 Gertrude Mantha, interview with the author, 11 January 2005 (p. 2).

13 Gertrude Mantha and Lorne Ray, interview with the author, 7 September 2004 (p. 2).

14 Gertrude Mantha, interview with the author, 28 February 2006 (p. 10).

15 Ibid.

16 Diane Ray-Parker, interview with the author, 6 May 2006 (pp. 3 & 4).

17 Gertrude Mantha, interview with the author, 7 September 2004 (p. 16).

18 Gertrude Mantha, interview with the author, 11 January 2005 (p. 11).

19 Patrick Mantha, interview with the author, 4 April 2006 (pp. 6 & 7).

20 See Appendix 4: *Amour immaculé/Immaculate Love.*

21 Gertrude Mantha, in prepared recordings, November 2004–March 2005.

22 Gertrude Mantha, interview with the author, 7 September 2004 (p. 20).

23 Gérard and Bernard Pelot, *Billings Bridge, Mon village, ma vie* (Gatineau: Ecrits d'or, 1999), p. 195.

24 Georgette Lamoureux, *Histoire d'Ottawa*, coll. *Histoire d'Ottawa*, Volume 4, p. 247.

25 Gertrude Mantha, interview with the author, 28 February 2006 (p. 10).

26 Georgette Bergeron, interview with the author, 5 May 2005 (p. 19).

27 Gertrude Mantha and Lorne Ray, interview with the author, 7 September 2004 (p. 14).

28   Gertrude Mantha, interview with the author, 1 April 2004 (p. 19).

29   Gertrude Mantha, interview with the author, 10 August 2006 (p. 13).

30   Gertrude Mantha, interview with the author, 1 April 2004 (p. 19).

31   Ibid., p. 7).

32   Ibid., p. 6).

33   Proverbs 17, 20.

Chapter 5

1   Gertude Mantha, interview with the author, 1 April 2004 (p. 4).

2   Gertrude Mantha, in a prepared recording, November 2004–March 2005, (p. 1).

3   Clothilde Bergeron, interview with the author, 4 May 2005 (p. 13).

4   Gertrude Mantha, interview with the author, 7 September 2004 (p. 18).

5   Gertrude Mantha, interview with the author, 28 February 2006 (p. 16).

6   Gertrude Mantha, in a prepared recording, November 2004–March 2005, (p. 3).

7   Gertrude Mantha, interview with the author, 28 February 2006 (p. 8).

8   Ibid., page 9

9   Allan Robertson, *Memories of Rideau Park*, unpublished manuscript, 12 July 2000, p. 6.

10   Gertrude Mantha and Lorne Ray, interview with the author, 7 September 2004 (p. 5).

11   Gertrude Mantha, interview with the author, 1 April 2004 (p. 6).

12   www.yesnet.yk.ca/schools/projects/canadianhistory/depression

13   Gertrude Mantha, interview with the author, 1 April 2004 (p. 7).

14   Gertrude Mantha, interview with the author, 28 February 2006 (p. 7), and 7 September (p. 16).

15   Gertrude Mantha, interview with the author, 2 May 2006 (pp. 5 & 6).

16   Gertrude Mantha, interview with the author, 28 February 2006 (p. 11).

17   Gertrude Mantha, interview with the author, 2 May 2006 (p. 5).

18   Gertrude Mantha, 7 September 2004 (p. 19) and 1 April 2004 (p. 16).

19   Gertrude Mantha, interview with the author, 1 April 2004 (p. 16).

20   Gertrude Mantha and Lorne Ray, interview with the author, 7 September 2004 (p. 18 & 19).

21   Gertrude Mantha, in a prepared recording, November 2004–March 2005; and in interview with the author, 7 September 2004 (p. 17).

22   Gertrude Mantha, interview with the author, 28 February 2006 (pp. 13 & 15), and 1 April 2004 (p. 16).

23   Gertrude Mantha, interview with the author, 1 April 2004 (p. 7).

24   Diane Ray-Parker, interview with the author, 6 May 2006 (p. 3).

25   Gertrude Mantha, interview with the author, 1 April 2004 (p. 4).

26   Gertrude Mantha, interview with the author, 8 April 2004 (p. 5).

27   Georgette Bergeron, interview with the author, 5 May 2005 (p. 1).

28   Gertrude Mantha, interview with the author, 10 August 2006 (p. 10).

29   Gertrude Mantha, interview with the author, 11 January 2005 (p. 4).

30   Gertrude Mantha, interview with the author, 28 February 2006 (p. 16 & 17).

31   Lamoureux, *Histoire d'Ottawa et de sa population française*, p. 64.

32   Gertrude Mantha, in a prepared recording, November 2004–March 2005; and interview with the author, 1 April 2004 (p. 6).

33   Gertrude Mantha, interview with the author, 28 February 2006 (p. 19).

34   Lamoureux, *Histoire d'Ottawa et de sa population française*, p. 45.

35   Gertrude Mantha and Lorne Ray, interview with the author, 7 September 2004 (p. 5).

36   Gertrude Mantha, interview with the author, 10 August 2006 (p. 5).

37   Frank Mansfield, interview with the author, 2006 (p. 10).

38   Gertrude Mantha, interview with the author, 2 May 2006 (p. 2).

39   http://www.bytown.net/depress.htm.

40   Gertrude Mantha, interview with the author, 29 March 2004 (p. 2).

41   Gertrude Mantha, in a prepared recording, November 2004–March 2005, interview with the author, 7 September 2004 (p. 2).

42 Gertrude Mantha and Lorne Ray, interview with the author, 7 September 2004 (p. 10).

43 Gertrude Mantha, in a prepared recording, November 2004–March 2005, (p. 4).

44 Gertrude Mantha, interview with the author, 8 April 2004 (p. 1).

45 Gertrude Mantha, interview with the author, 7 September 2004 (p. 21), and 11 January 2005 (p. 9).

46 Gertrude Mantha, in a prepared recording, November 2004–March 2005 (p. 9).

47 Gertrude Mantha, interview with the author, 1 April 2004 (p. 12).

48 Ibid., p. 15).

49 Recording prepared by Gertrude Mantha, November 2004–March 2005 (p. 4).

Chapter 6

1   Gertrude Mantha, interview with the author, 10 August 2006 (pp. 1 & 2).

2   Alfred Emery, Bulletin paroissial de Paincourt, 1914, as told by Amédée Emery, in *Villages et visages de l'Ontario français* by René Brodeur and Robert Choquette (Ontario Office of Distance Education, 1979), p. 89.

3   Gertrude Mantha, interview with the author, 10 August 2006 (p. 3).

4   Gertrude Mantha, interview with the author, 29 November 2005 (pp. 12–13).

5   Gertrude Mantha, interview with the author, 2 May 2006 (p. 10).

6   Gertrude Mantha, interview with the author, 1 April 2004 (p. 9).

7   Gertrude Mantha, interview with the author, 2 May 2006 (p. 12).

8   Ibid.

9   Gertrude Mantha, interview with the author, 29 November 2005 (p. 13).

10 Lamoureux, *Histoire d'Ottawa et sa population canadienne-française*, p. 147.

11 Gertrude Mantha, interview with the author, 7 September 2004 (p. 8).

12 Gertrude Mantha, interview with the author, 1 April 2004 (p. 8).

13 Gertrude Mantha, interview with the author, 2 May 2006 (p. 8).

14 Gertrude Mantha, interview with the author, 29 November 2005 (pp. 8–9).

15 Lamoureux, *Histoire d'Ottawa et sa population canadienne-française*, p. 169.

16 Ibid., p. 170.

17 Gertrude Mantha, interview with the author, 8 April 2004 (p. 7).

18 Gertrude Mantha, interview with the author, 29 November 2005 (pp. 13 & 14).

19 DesNeiges Bergeron, interview with the author, 4 May 2005 (pp. 1 & 3).

20 Ibid., p. 6).

21 Lamoureux, *Histoire d'Ottawa et sa population canadienne-française*, pp. 189 & 192.

22 Gertrude Mantha and Lorne Ray, interview with the author, 7 September 2004 (p. 9).

Chapter 7

1   Correspondence with Albert Mantha.

2   Christina Ray-Richardson, interview with the author, 25 May 2006 (p. 6).

3   Pauline Mantha, interview with the author, 29 April 2006 (p. 1).

4   Louise Mantha, interview with the author, 20 September 2004 (p. 3).

5   Diane Ray-Parker, interview with the author, 6 May 2006 (p. 11).

6   Louise Mantha, interview with the author, 20 September 2004 (p. 3).

7   David Ray, interview with the author, 8 July 2005 (p. 2).

8   Louise Mantha, interview with the author, 20 September 2004 (p. 2).

9   Gertrude Mantha, interview with the author, 2 May 2006 (p. 6).

10 David Ray, interview with the author, 8 July 2005 (p. 2).

11 Patrick Mantha, interview with the author, 4 April 2006 (p. 8).

12 Louise Mantha, interview with the author, 20 September 2004 (p. 6).

13 Cathy Ray-Steele, interview with the author, 30 January 2006 (p. 4).

14 Gertrude and Lorne, interview with the author, 7 September 2004 (p. 11).

15 Louise Mantha, interview with the author, 20 September 2004 (pp. 3 & 6).

16 Ibid. (p. 4).

17 Note written by Betty Fleming and given to Gertrude Mantha.

18 David Ray, interview with the author, 8 July 2005 (p. 2).

19 E-mail from Donald Ray.

20 Diane Ray-Parker, interview with the author, 6 May 2006 (p. 11).

21 Pauline Mantha, interview with the author, 29 April 2006 (p. 1).

22 Ibid. (p. 5).

23 Anne Mantha Letellier, interview with the author, 22 February 2006 (p. 1).

24 Sophie Feodorovna Rostopchine (1799–1874), author born in St Petersburg and renowned for the series of stories she wrote for her grandchildren. She married Count Eugène de Ségur.

25 Diane Ray-Parker, interview with the author, 6 May 2006 (p. 7).

26 Suzanne Mantha Fourcassié, interview with the author, 17 October 2005 (p. 4).

27 From a letter from Patrick Mantha, July 2007.

28 David Ray, interview with the author, 8 July 2005 (p. 3).

29 Louise Mantha, interview with the author, 20 September 2004 (p. 4).

30 Suzanne Mantha Fourcassié, interview with the author, 17 October 2005 (p. 1).

31 Cathy Ray-Steele, interview with the author, 30 January 2006 (pp. 8 & 9).

32 Gertrude Mantha, interview with the author, 1 April 2004 (p. 10).

Chapter 8

1 Georgette Bergeron, interview with the author, 5 May 2005 (p. 7).

2 Ibid.

3 Clothilde Bergeron, interview with the author, 4 May 2005 (p. 2).

4 Georgette Bergeron, interview with the author, 5 May 2005 (p. 13).

5 Ibid., p. 17).

6 The whole story of the trip to the Yukon is taken from the interview betweem Clothilde Bergeron and the author.

Chapter 9

1 Cathy Ray-Steele, interview with the author, 30 January 2006 (p. 1).

2   Ibid. (p. 4).

3   Ibid. (p. 5).

4   Ibid. (p. 1).

5   Jean-Pierre Mantha, interview with the author, 1 May 2006 (p. 2).

6   Patrick Mantha, interview with the author, 4 April 2006 (pp. 9 & 19).

7   Louise Mantha, interview with the author, 20 September 2004 (p. 4).

8   Suzanne Mantha Fourcassié, interview with the author, 17 October 2005 (p. 3).

9   Louise Mantha, interview with the author, 20 September 2004 (p. 7).

10 Gertrude Mantha, interview with the author, 10 August 2006 (pp. 3 & 4).

11 Diane Ray-Parker, interview with the author, 6 May 2006 (p. 18).

Chapter 10

1   Christina Ray-Richardson, interview with the author, 25 May 2006 (p. 5).

2   Anne Mantha-Letellier, interview with the author, 22 February 2006 (p. 1).

3   Cathy Ray-Steele, interview with the author, 30 January 2006 (p. 1).

4   Louise Mantha, interview with the author, 20 September 2004 (p. 3).

5   Ibid.

6   Cathy Ray-Steele, interview with the author, 30 January 2006 (p. 2).

7   Pauline Mantha, interview with the author, 29 April 2006 (p. 1).

8   Donald Ray, interview with the author, 2006 (p. 1).

9   Louise Mantha, interview with the author, 20 September 2004 (p. 9).

10 Ibid., p. 11).

11 Christina Ray-Richardson, interview with the author, 25 May 2006 (p. 1).

12 "D & C" means "dilation and curetage," a medical procedure.

13 Diane Ray-Parker, interview with the author, 6 May 2006 (p. 19).

14 Ibid.

15 Suzanne Mantha, interview with the author, 17 October 2005 (p. 7).

BIBLIOGRAPHY

Abbott, Elizabeth, *Une histoire des maîtresses*, Editions Fides, 2004, 617 pp. (ISBN 2-7621-2494-8)

Allaire, Chanoine J.B.A., *Dictionnaire biographique du clergé canadien-français*, compléments 1, Montréal, Imprimerie de la "Croix", 1928.

Bédard, Roméo, abbé. *History Montmartre, Sask.* 1893–1953. Regina, diocèse de Regina, 1953. I found a copy of this unpublished document in the Saskatchewan Archives Board in Regina.

Black, Norman Fergus. *History of Saskatchewan and The Old North West*, North West Historical Company Publishers, 1913, 605 pp.

Brault, Lucien Dr., *Ottawa, capitale du Canada de ses débuts à nos jours*, Université d'Ottawa, 1942, 311 pp.

Broadfoot, Barry. *Ten Lost Years 1929–1939, Memories of Canadians Who Survived the Depression*, McClelland & Stewart Ltd., 1997, 436 pp. (ISBN 0-7710-1652-2)

Brodeur, René et Robert Choquette. *Villages et visages de l'Ontario français*, Office de la télécommunication éducative de l'Ontario, 1979, 142 pp. (ISBN 2-7621-0747-4)

Dumont, Micheline, Michèle Jean, Marie Lavigne et Jennifer Stoddart. *L'histoire des femmes au Québec depuis quatre siècles*, Le Collectif Clio, Les Quinze, éditeur, 1982, 521 pp. (ISBN 2-89026-309-6)

Emery, Alfred, *Bulletin paroissial de Paincourt*, 1914, relaté par Amédée Emery et cité dans *Villages et visages de l'Ontario français* de René Brodeur et Robert Choquette, Office de la télécommunication éducative de l'Ontario, 1979, p. 89.

Farmers and Business Directory for the counties of Haliburton, Peterboro and Victoria and the districts of Muskoka, Parry Sound, Nipissing, Manitoulin, Rainy River, Thunder Bay and Keewatin. 1906–7, Vol. XIV, Union Publishing Company of Ingersoll, 1906, p. 536.

Fédération des Femmes Canadiennes-françaises de la paroisse St-Jacques de Hanmer, Ont. *Pionnières de chez-nous*, Les Éditions de l'Ami du Peuple, juin 1982 et octobre 1982. Documents historiques numéros 76 and 77 de la Société Historique du Nouvel-Ontario, 156 pp.

Frémont, Donatien. *Les Français dans l'Ouest Canadien*, Les Cahiers d'histoire, Numéro 1, La Société historique de Saint-Boniface, 1980, 163 pp. (ISBN 0-920640-24-9)

Frenette, Pierre. *Histoire des Escoumins. Un siècle et demi d'enracinement*, Société historique de la Côte-Nord, Sites et villages nord-côtiers, no 7, Bibliothèque nationale du Québec, 1996, 88 pp. (ISBN 2-9800993-7-6)

Gaudreau, Guy. "Les activités forestières dans deux communautés agricoles du Nouvel-Ontario, 1900–1920." *Revue d'histoire de l'Amérique française*, Département d'histoire, Université Laurentienne, pp 501–529.

Gerein, Frank. *Golden Jubilee, Archdiocese of Regina 1911–1961*,* Outline History of the Archdiocese of Regina written and compiled on the occasion of its Golden jubilee Year. Imprimatur, M.C. O'Neill, Archbishop of Regina, 23 September 1961, 269 pp.

*Comment: This book contains certain factual errors.

For example, on page 140 it states that Father J.A. Roy was named the first curate of St Anne's parish in Wolseley in 1882. However this cannot be right since he was only ordained in 1888.

Another example: The author notes on page 142 that the Sacré Cœur parish in Montmartre was established in 1893 by a small group of French Canadians but in fact it was by a group of immigrants from France brought over by Mr. de Trémaudan.

Gray, Charlotte. *Canada, A Portrait in Letters*, Charlotte Gray, 2003, Anchor Canada edition 2004, 536 pp.

Hémon, Louis. *Maria Chapdelaine*, Ed. de luxe illustrée par Fernand Labelle, Éditions Fides, 1994, 234 pp. (ISBN 2-7621-1764-x)

Huel, Raymond Joseph Armand. *Archbishop A.-A. Taché of St.Boniface: the "good fight" and the illusive vision.* Edmonton: University of Alberta Press, 2003. xxv, 429 pp. (ISBN 088864-406-x)

Lamoureux, Georgette. *Histoire d'Ottawa et sa population canadienne-française*, Tome IV, 1900–1926. Canada 1984 par G. Lamoureux, 321 pp.

Lamoureux, Georgette. *Histoire d'Ottawa et sa population canadienne-française*, Tome V, 1926–1950, Canada 1989 par G.Lamoureux, 327 pp.

La Sainte Bible, Editions de Maredsous, octobre 1951, 303 pp.

Leaning, John. *The Story of the Glebe*, John Leaning, October 1999, 67 pp. (ISBN 0-9685030-0-4)

LeBelle, Wayne F., *Valley East* 1850–2002, Journal Printers, Sudbury ON, (no date), 355 pp. (ISBN 0-9699362-2-2)

LeBlanc, Jean. *Dictionnaire biographique des évêques catholiques du Canada*, Collection Gratianus, Wilson & Lafleur Ltée, Montréal, 2002, 881 pp. (ISBN 2-89127-560-8)

Le Canada Écclésiastique, Annuaire du Clergé, Montréal, publié par la Cie Cadieux & Derome pour les volumes couvrant les années avant 1910 et par la Librairie Beauchemin Ltée pour les volumes à partir de 1910.

McEvoy Rooney, Joan. *Historic Homes and Buildings of the Billings Bridge Community, a Self-Guided Tour*, The Association of Friends of the Billings Estate Museum, 2004, 29 pp. (ISBN 0-9736658-0-7)

Might Directories Limited. 1919. *Might Directory* for 1918 and 1919. (Ottawa, Might Directories, Ltd. On microfilm in the City of Ottawa Archives.

Parent, Huguette. *Hanmer*, Dans la série PRO-F-ONT, Ottawa, Centre Franco-Ontarien de Ressources Pédagogiques, 1980, 166 pp.

Parent, Huguette. *Le Township de Hanmer 1904–1969*, Document historique No 70, La Société Historique du Nouvel-Ontario, Université de Sudbury, 1979, 51 pp.

Parish Register of Baptisms, Marriages and Deaths, St. Anne Roman Catholic Church, Wolseley, Sask. (Includes Missions of Qu'Appelle, Balgonie, Wolseley, Grenfell and Broadview) 1888–1905, Loaned for microfilming by Rev. F. Marcotte, St. Anne Church, Wolseley, Sask. April 1964. The microfilm is at the Saskatchewan Archives Board in Regina, Saskatchewan.

Pelot, Gérard et Bernard, *Billings Bridge, Mon village, ma vie*, Les Ecrits d'or, Gatineau, Québec, 1999, 225 pp.

Robertson, Allan. M*emories of Rideau Park*. Unpublished, 12 July 2000, 8 pp.

Sudbury Journal, Sudbury Public Library.

Taylor, John H., *Ottawa, An Illustrated History*, Canadian Museum of Civilization, 1986, 232 pp. (ISBN 0-88862-981-8)

Tremblay, Emilian Milton. C.S.S.R., *The Epic of St. Anne in Western Canada*, Imprimatur Andrew Roborecki, Ukrainian Catholic Bishop of Saskatchewan, 8 June 1967, 318 pp.

Internet Sites

Dioscese of Sault Ste. Marie: Paroisse St-Jacque: Historique de la paroisse Saint-Jacques, Hanmer, Ontario, 1905–1923. http://stjacques.diocesessm.org/about/history/fr

Government of Canada. Canada's Digital Collection/Les Collections Numérisées du Canada. http://collections.ic.gc.ca

Great Depression of Canada. http://www.yesnet.yk.ca/schools/projects/canadianhistory/depression/depression.html

Lalonde, André. Les Canadiens français de l'Ouest: espoirs, tragédies, incertitude. http://www.cefan.ulaval.ca/franco/my_html/LALONDE.html

Les Escoumins. http://www.escoumins.ca/escoumins/page.php?section=25

Les Labelles/The Labelles. http://www.leslabelle.com/genealogie/genealogie.asp

Library and Archives Canada/Bibliotheque et Archives Canada: Canadian Confederation. http://www.collectionscanada.gc.ca/confederation/index-e.html

Saskatchewan Settlement Experience. http://sasksettlement.com

Société historique de la Saskatchewan: Musées virtuels. http://www.societehisto.com/musees_virtuels_n277.html

The Great Depression and Its Affects on Ottawa. http://www.bytown.net/depress.htm

The Manitoba Historical Society: Transactions of the Manitoba Historical Society. http://www.mhs.mb.ca/docs/transactions

Wikipédia: Alexandre-Antonin Taché. http://fr.wikipedia.org/wiki/Alexandre-Antonin_Taché

Wikipédia: Histoire du Manitoba. http://fr.wikipedia.org/wiki/Catégorie:Histoire_du_Manitoba

Wikipédia: Rébellion de la rivière-Rouge. http://fr.wikipedia.org/wiki/R%C3%A9bellion_de_la_rivi%C3%A8re_Rouge

Wikipédia: Rébellion du Nord-Ouest. http://fr.wikipedia.org/wiki/Rébellion_du_Nord-Ouest

Index

A

activités forestières dans deux communautés agricoles du Nouvel-Ontario, Les (Gaudreau), 186–187
Adam, Alice, 119
Air Canada, 113
Amour Immaculé (Nelligan), 189

B

Baker family, 85, 86, 92, 93, 94, 95
Balgonie, Saskatchewan, 23, 25
Bambi, 139
Bank Street, 92–94
baptismal certificate
  of Désiré Jérémie Roy, 21, 24–25, 31, 191
  of Marie-Louise Bouchard, 3–5, 191
Barbe, Serge, 203
Beaulieu, Albina, 152
Beaulieu, Henri, 13, 183
Bédard, Abbot Roméo, 19
Bennett, Albert, 85, 102
Bergeron, Claire-Hilda. *See* Labelle, Claire-Hilda
Bergeron, Clothilde
  on the Hanmer homestead, 9
  on J.A. Roy as Joseph, 31
  on Marie-Louise, 74, 153–156
  on Napoléon Labelle, 14

  on Napoléon's reaction to Marie-Louise's departure, 43
Bergeron, DesNeiges, 8, 119–120
Bergeron, Florian, 151–152, 154
Bergeron, Georgette
  graduation, 149
  on J.A. Roy's return to the Church, 89
  on Marie-Louise and J.A. Roy, 36–37
  on Napoléon and Georgianne, 5–6
  on Napoléon Labelle, 15
  on Napoléon's reaction to Marie-Louise's departure, 44
  photo, 150
  on priests and guns, 64
  shopping with Marie-Louise, 139
  the two gossips and, 150–152, 153–156
Bernard (dog), 105–106
Berthierville, Quebec, 21, 123
Bey, Auguste de, 42
Billings Bridge, 51, 62, 93, 96
Billings family, 64
Birds, The, (Hitchcock), 139
birth certificate. *See* baptismal certificate
birth control, 42
Blezard Valley, 85, 100
bloomers, 166–167
Bolen, Rev. Donald, 201
Bouchard, Jean, 5
Bouchard, Théophile, 4–6

225